Preface

Are you a health professional who wishes to improve the quality of your practice using systematic reviews? Are you embarking on a career in public health, epidemiology or health technology assessment? Are you about to start your first review? If so, this book is for you. It describes the main principles behind systematic reviews of healthcare research and provides guidance on how reviews can be appraised, conducted and applied in practice.

As our current healthcare practice and policy increasingly relies on clear and comprehensive summaries of information collated through systematic literature reviews, it is necessary for us to understand how reviews and practice guidelines are produced. You may not be trained in health research methods, but this book will enable you to grasp the principles behind reviewing literature. In this way you will be able to critically appraise published systematic reviews and guidelines, and evaluate their inferences and recommendations for application in your practice.

Published reviews and guidelines are not always adequate or sufficient for our needs. Have you ever wondered how you could conduct your own review? The resources required for undertaking reviews are increasingly becoming available in a clinical setting. The appointment of clinical librarians, Internet access to many journals, ease of obtaining interlibrary loans and the availability of user-friendly software make it possible for systematic reviews to be conducted by healthcare practitioners. This book highlights the core information necessary for planning and preparing reviews. It focuses on a clinical readership and new reviewers, not on experienced epidemiologists and statisticians. Using this book you will be able to initiate your own review.

For too many years there has been a mystery surrounding systematic reviews and reviewers. How did they select certain studies and reject others? What did they do to pool results? How did a bunch of insignificant findings suddenly become significant? You are about to embark on a journey that will demystify these intrigues. Enjoy reading.

KS Khan,
R Kunz,
J Kleijnen
and G Antes
October 2002

Systematic Reviews to Support Evidence-based Medicine:

how to review and apply findings of healthcare research

Khalid S Khan
Regina Kunz
Jos Kleijnen
Gerd Antes

The ROYAL
SOCIETY *of*
MEDICINE
PRESS *Limited*

LIVERPOOL
JOHN MOORES UNIVERSITY
AVRIL ROBARTS LRC
TITHEBARN STREET
LIVERPOOL L2 2ER
TEL. 0151 231 4022

LIVERPOOL JMU LIBRARY

3 1111 01095 0895

©2003 Royal Society of Medicine Press Ltd
Reprinted 2004
1 Wimpole Street, London W1G 0AE, UK
207 E Westminster Road, Lake Forest, IL 60045, USA
www.rsmpress.co.uk

Apart from any fair dealing for the purposes of research or private study,
criticism or review, as permitted under the UK Copyright Designs and Patents
Act, 1988, no part of this publication may be reproduced, stored or
transmitted, in any form or by any means, without the prior permission in
writing of the publishers or in the case of reprographic reproduction in
accordance with the terms of licences issued by the Copyright Licensing
Agency in the UK, or in accordance with the terms of licences issued by the
appropriate Reproduction Rights Organization outside the UK. Enquiries
concerning reproduction outside the terms stated here should be sent to the
publishers at the UK address printed on this page.

The rights of Khalid S Khan, Regina Kunz, Jos Kleijnen and Gerd Antes to
be identified as authors of this work has been asserted by them in accordance
with the Copyright, Designs and Patents Act, 1998.

British Library Cataloguing in Publication Data
A catalogue record for this book is available from the British Library

ISBN 1-85315-525-X

Typeset by Phoenix Photosetting, Chatham, Kent
Printed in Europe by the Alden Group, Oxford

About the authors

Together we are veterans of over 150 systematic reviews. Over the years we have worked with healthcare commissioners, clinicians and other decision makers, producing reviews to inform policy and practice. We have collaborated with other epidemiologists and statisticians to advance methods for undertaking systematic reviews. Two of us work in an academic setting producing and promoting systematic reviews; two of us work in a clinical setting with patients, applying evidence from reviews to inform our practice.

Khalid S Khan, an Obstetrician-Gynaecologist at the Birmingham Women's Hospital, UK, is a clinician trained in systematic reviews and evidence-based medicine (EBM). Qualified in medical education he is also Clinical Sub-dean and Associate Director of the Education Resource Centre at his hospital where he runs a journal club and other EBM activities, including evidence-supported ward rounds and workshops on critical appraisal. Alongside his clinical routine he leads a number of systematic review projects and clinical trials, teaches undergraduates and postgraduates and provides peer review analysis for several clinical journals. He is also an honorary member at the Horten Centre, University of Zürich, which aims to disseminate EBM. In 2000, a senior secondment at the Centre for Reviews and Dissemination (CRD), York, UK, brought him an opportunity to update the CRD Report 4 on 'Undertaking Systematic Reviews of Research on Effectiveness'. This book was conceived during his time in York.

Regina Kunz practices Nephrology at the Charité, Berlin, and is a senior scientist at the German Cochrane Centre, Freiburg. She is one of those few clinicians who have been formally trained in clinical epidemiology and systematic reviews. She is a founding member of the German EBM Network and also runs the EBM Reference Centre of the Rheumatology Competence Network in Germany. She has participated in the design of the German National EBM Curriculum and has run many courses in systematic reviews and EBM. She is a member of the Editorial Board of the Journal of Continuing Education and Quality Assurance (*Zeitschrift für Aerztliche Fortbildung und Qualitaetssicherung*) and has edited *Textbook of EBM* (*Lehrbuch der Evidenzbasierten Medizin*, Deutscher Aerzteverlag 2000).

Jos Kleijnen is the Director of the Centre for Reviews and Dissemination, York, UK. Following his graduation from medical school, he pursued a career as a clinical epidemiologist and has a wealth of experience in conducting and disseminating systematic reviews and other research. He is a member of various steering groups and advisory committees for commissioners of systematic reviews. He was the founding Director of the Dutch Cochrane Centre and is a member of several Methods Working Groups of the Cochrane Collaboration. He is an editor of the Cochrane Peripheral

Vascular Diseases Review Group and also runs and participates in courses on systematic reviews and EBM in several countries. This includes a collaboration with the Horten Centre in Zürich, Switzerland.

Gerd Antes is the Director of the German Cochrane Centre, Freiburg. He is a medical statistician and has in-depth knowledge of the mathematics behind meta-analyses, heterogeneity, funnel plots, etc. As well as his interests in methodological work, statistical computing and medical informatics, he set up the German Cochrane initiative and spends considerable time supporting the progress of EBM and systematic reviews in Germany. He is a founding member and Speaker of the German EBM Network. He has been a member of the Cochrane Collaboration Steering Group for several years.

We have put this book together because we feel that health professionals have much to gain from reviews and guidelines and at the same time reviews and guidelines have much to gain from them. With this book we hope healthcare practitioners will feel empowered to use reviews effectively and to initiate their own reviews.

Acknowledgements

No work can ever be completed without the support of many individuals. The authors are grateful to Susan Hahné, Anjum Doshani, Peter J Thompson and Jack Cohen for their critical review of an earlier version of this book; Mary Publicover for her review of Step 2; Christine Anne Clark and Anne-Marie Bagnall for their review of case study 1; and Sue O'Meara for her review of case study 3.

Contents

List of abbreviations

CDSR	Cochrane Database of Systematic Reviews
CENTRAL	Cochrane Central Register of Controlled Trials
CER	control event rate
CI	confidence interval
DARE	Database of Abstracts of Reviews of Effects
EBM	evidence-based medicine
EER	experimental event rate
ES	effect size (for continuous data)
HTA	health technology assessment
ITT	intention-to-treat analysis
LR	likelihood ratio (LR+, LR for positive test result; LR-, LR for negative test result)
MeSH	medical subject heading
NNT	number needed to treat
OR	odds ratio *(not to be confused with Boolean operator OR used in searching literature electronically)*
RCT	randomized controlled trial
RD	risk difference (or ARR, absolute risk reduction)
RR	relative risk
SD	standard deviation
SE	standard error

Introduction

We hardly ever come across a healthcare journal that does not publish reviews. What makes them ubiquitous? Reviews provide summaries of evidence contained in a number of individual studies on a specific topic. Research that is relevant to our practice is scattered all over the literature and sometimes it is published in languages foreign to us. By going through a single review article in our own language we can get a quick overview of a wide range of evidence on a particular topic. Therefore, we like reviews. They provide us with a way of keeping up-to-date without the trouble of having to go through the individual studies relevant to our practice. With an ever-increasing number of things to do in our professional lives and not enough time to do them, who wouldn't find reviews handy? In all honesty, even if we had the time and means to identify and appraise relevant studies, many of us would still prefer reviews.

Now a word of warning – the manner in which traditional reviews search for studies, collate evidence and generate inferences is often suspect. In the worst cases, personal interests of the author may drive the whole of the review process and its conclusions. After all, many of the reviews we read are invited commentaries, they are not properly conducted pieces of research. So how can we be certain that reviews are not misleading us? This is why systematic reviews have come to replace traditional reviews.

Robust systematic reviews of healthcare literature are proper pieces of research. They identify relevant studies, appraise their quality and summarize their results using scientific methodology. In this way they differ from traditional reviews and off-the-cuff commentaries produced by 'experts'. More importantly, the recommendations of systemtic reviews, instead of reflecting personal views of 'experts', are based on balanced inferences generated from the collated evidence.

This book describes the principles behind systematically reviewing the literature on effects of health care. Using this book, readers should be able to confidently appraise a review for its quality, as well as initiate one of their own.

A **systematic review** is a research article that identifies relevant studies, appraises their quality and summarizes their results using a scientific methodology.

The term **meta-analysis** is not synonymous with a **systematic review**. It is only a part of the **review**. It is a statistical technique for combining the results of a number of individual studies to produce a summary result. Some publications called meta-analysis are not systematic reviews.

From here onwards whenever this book uses the term **review** it will mean a **systematic review**, using these terms interchangeably. Reviews should never be done in any other way.

Critically appraising systematic reviews

What is involved in the identification, appraisal and application of evidence summarized in reviews?

Framing questions
|
Identifying relevant reviews
|
Assessing quality of the review and its evidence
|
Summarizing the evidence
|
Interpreting the findings

Evidence-based medicine (EBM) is the judicious use of current best evidence in making decisions about health care. Systematic reviews provide strong evidence to underpin EBM.

Guidelines are systematically developed statements to assist practitioners and patients in making decisions about specific clinical situations. They often, but not always, use evidence from systematic reviews.

More and more healthcare policy is being based on clear and comprehensive summaries of information collated through systematic reviews of the relevant literature. So, in the current day and age, evidence-based practice requires more than just critical appraisal of individual studies. Practice guidelines are a prime example of how systematic reviews have come to occupy a pivotal role in our professional lives.

Systematic reviews may represent a quantum leap in review methodology. However, we should not have blind faith. Reviews and guidelines, just like individual studies, can be of a variable quality. There are numerous examples of poor reviews published in top healthcare journals and of inferior guidelines produced by professional bodies. Hence, there is a potential for misleading inferences even among apparently robust reviews and guidelines. Therefore it is necessary for us, as healthcare practitioners, to acquire a deeper understanding of the principles behind systematic reviews. Although we may only have a basic knowledge in health research methods and consider the task of appraising reviews onerous, with this book readers will be able to grasp the process and pitfalls of systematically reviewing literature, and discriminate between robust and not-so-robust reviews and guidelines more easily.

We can identify existing reviews to support our practice by searching the resources shown in Box 0.1. Once relevant reviews have been identified, the quality of their methods should be appraised, their evidence should be examined and their findings should be assessed for application in practice. Examples of how to use findings from existing reviews are shown in the case studies in Section B of this book. When drawing on reviews to support our practice, we will occasionally become painfully aware that relevant reviews either do not exist or they supply inadequate information. When we can't find a review that meets our needs, why not initiate a new one?

Conducting a systematic review

Internet access to literature searching, the ability to obtain articles either electronically or through interlibrary loans, user-friendly software for meta-analysis, etc. all make this new kind of reviewing possible. As these resources are increasingly available in a

Box 0.1 Selected sources of systematic reviews and guidelines

The Cochrane Library* (www.cochrane.org)

It has several databases of published and ongoing reviews:

- **The Cochrane Database of Systematic Reviews (CDSR)**
  Contains the full text of regularly updated systematic reviews of healthcare interventions carried out by the Cochrane Collaboration, plus protocols for reviews currently in preparation.
- **Database of Abstracts of Reviews of Effects (DARE)⁺**
  Critical appraisals of systematic reviews found in sources other than CDSR. These reviews are identified by regular searching of bibliographic databases, hand searching of key major medical journals, and by scanning grey literature.
- **Health Technology Assessment (HTA) Database⁺**
  Abstracts of completed technology assessments and ongoing projects being conducted by members of the International Network of Agencies for Health Technology Assessment (INAHTA) and other healthcare technology agencies. Most of these include systematic reviews.
- **Collaborative Review Groups (CRGs)**
  Found under 'about the Cochrane Collaboration' in the Cochrane Library. It contains a list of the total output of each one of 50 CRGs and provides an alternative method of searching the Cochrane Library.

There are more systematic reviews around than one might think. For example, in the 4th issue of the 2002 Cochrane Library alone there were 1519 complete reviews and 1136 protocols of reviews in CDSR, 2940 abstracts of quality assessed reviews in DARE and 2838 abstracts of technology assessments in the HTA database.

General electronic databases: (*also see Box 2.3*)
- MEDLINE – PubMed Clinical Queries using the Systematic Reviews feature available at www.ncbi.nlm.nih.gov/entrez/query/static/clinical.html
  At the time of writing there were 53 593 citations in the PubMed Systematic Reviews subset strategy.
- CINAHL, EMBASE, PsycLIT and others may be searched for reviews adapting one of the search filters (a combination of text words, indexing terms and subject headings that captures relevant articles) from the Centre for Reviews and Dissemination search strategies available at www.york.ac.uk/inst/crd/search.htm

Selected Internet sites:
- CMA Infobase – www.cma.ca/cpgs/
- Guidelines and Guidelines in Practice – www.eguidelines.co.uk
- Health services/technology assessment text (HSTAT) – http://hstat.nlm.nih.gov/
- National Coordinating Centre for Health Technology Assessment – www.hta.nhsweb.nhs.uk/
- National Electronic Library for Health – www.nelh.nhs.uk/
- National Institute for Clinical Excellence (NICE) – www.nice.org.uk/
- National Guidelines Clearinghouse – www.guideline.gov/index.asp
- OMNI – http://omni.ac.uk (use advanced search and specify Practice Guidelines in Resource Type)
- ScHARR-Lock's Guide to the evidence – www.shef.ac.uk/uni/academic/R-Z/scharr/ir/scebm.html
- SIGN guidelines – www.show.scot.nhs.uk/sign/home.htm
- Turning Research Into Practice (TRIP) – www.tripdatabase.com/

Selected print publications:
- Clinical Evidence – www.clinicalevidence.org
- Effective Health Care Bulletins – www.york.ac.uk/inst/crd/ehcb.htm

* See case study 1 for an example search of the Cochrane Library
⁺ also available free at www.york.ac.uk/inst/crd

Websites are constantly changing – the addresses provided in this book were obtained from searches in August to September 2002.

clinical setting, undertaking systematic reviews has become a realistic option for healthcare practitioners. But why should practitioners undertake reviews?

There is no shortage of reasons for undertaking one's own review. One may wish to conduct reviews for:

- supporting evidence-based practice
- personal professional development
- informing clinical policy
- publishing in a peer-reviewed journal
- writing an introduction to a research thesis
- preparing a presentation in a conference
- a technical report
- an invited commentary.

However, there should be no need to reinvent the wheel. Existing reviews and guidelines should be used to their full potential. Up-to-date good quality reviews may already contain all the information we need.

When reviews and guidelines on a specific topic do not exist, are not up-to-date or are of a poor quality, our options are:

- ask 'experts' for advice
- appraise available primary studies
- conduct a systematic review.

The **Cochrane Collaboration** is an international collaboration that aims to help with informed decision-making about health care by preparing, maintaining and increasing accessibility of systematic reviews of interventions. (www.cochrane.org)

A **Cochrane review** is a systematic review undertaken following the methodology of the **Cochrane Collaboration** and will be included in the **Cochrane Library**.

We realize that 'expert' opinions may not be evidence-based and they may be unacceptable to others – for every 'expert' there is an equal and opposite 'expert'. We know that appraisal of individual studies will not provide information on the complete picture. Isn't this the point where we want to start a new review? Many Cochrane reviews commence in this way and when they are published everyone can benefit from them. Conducting a new systematic review will take a lot of effort, but not everything that is worthwhile is easy.

When undertaking research projects, advanced courses or educational assignments, we (or at least our supervisors) should be aware that non-systematic reviews are increasingly less acceptable. Where do we go next? We should do our own systematic review. As academics in the health professions (without advanced epidemiology and statistics training), we may be used to publishing editorials, opinions and commentaries. We are now under pressure from journal editors to be more systematic in our approach. Why not try a systematic review for the next commentary? We may feel inhibited as the knowledge or skills required for initiating such reviews may not be within our grasp. Help is in our hands. This book provides the core information necessary for planning and initiating reviews of healthcare literature.

This book focuses primarily on a clinical readership and first-time reviewers, not on epidemiologists and statisticians. This book will enable readers to initiate reviews without relying on professional reviewers and will also give advice about further reading and how to seek professional input in difficult areas. Considering the nature of work involved in the various steps of a review, it is advisable to find one or more other reviewers to join in. First-time reviewers might want to attend a local workshop or course on systematic reviews. The Cochrane Collaboration organizes many of these – why not ask the local Cochrane Centre about their next training event?

How this book is structured

This book will help readers to understand the principles of systematic reviews. In the discourse that follows there is a step-by-step explanation of the review process. There are just five steps. This book provides guidance for each step of a review with examples from published reviews. Many examples are followed through the different steps so that we will be able to see the link between the steps. In addition, application of the theory is illustrated through case studies. Each case consists of a scenario requiring evidence from reviews, a demonstration of some review methods and a proposed resolution of the scenario. Insight into critical appraisal and conducting a systematic review can be gained by working through the various steps, examples and case studies.

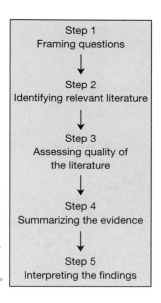

If we have made up our mind to initiate a review, we should first produce a brief outline (or a protocol) of the project containing some background information, and a specification of the problem to be addressed along with the methodology to be used in the review. Throughout the review work, the protocol will remind us where we are coming from and what direction we want to go in, avoiding distractions and keeping us on track. It will also provide a document that could be peer reviewed before the review work is commenced. Some people suggest that a review protocol should be posted on a website to facilitate a wide peer review, but input from visitors to the site may be variable. Realistically, we have a much better chance of getting a professional to comment on the protocol if we ask a colleague experienced in reviewing or if we register our review with a relevant Review Group of the Cochrane Collaboration.

This book will be a useful companion in protocol development as well as throughout the five steps in the review process:

- First, the problems to be addressed have to be specified in the form of well-structured questions (Step 1). This is a key step, as all other aspects of the review follow directly from the questions.
- Second, thorough literature searches have to be conducted to identify potentially

relevant studies that can shed light on the questions (Step 2). This is an essential feature that makes a review systematic.

- Third, the quality of the selected studies is assessed (Step 3).
- Fourth, the evidence concerning study characteristics and results is summarized (Step 4). When feasible and appropriate, statistical meta-analysis helps in collating the results.
- Finally, inferences and recommendations for practice are generated by interpreting and exploring the clinical relevance of the findings (Step 5).

> This book will focus mainly on reviews of research, examining the effects of interventions or exposures on health.

The key points about appraisal and conduct of reviews are summarized at the end of each step in Section A. The case studies in Section B illustrate the application of the review theory that is covered in the five steps. Readers may prefer to assimilate the review theory before turning to the case studies or they may read them in conjunction with the information contained in Section A. A 'suggested reading' list provides references to direct readers to other texts for theoretical and methodological issues that are beyond the core material covered in this book.

The guidance in this book is pitched at a level suitable for users of systematic reviews and for novice reviewers. It should not be seen as providing a 'set menu' for appraising and undertaking systematic reviews. What it offers is a range of 'à la carte' guidance, which can be applied flexibly depending on the question and context.

Key points about this book

- This book will enable readers to confidently appraise published reviews for their quality, as well as to initiate their own reviews.
- It describes the main principles behind systematically reviewing literature on the effects of health care, focusing on a readership of healthcare professionals.
- It includes a step-by-step explanation of how to appraise and conduct reviews along with illustrative examples and case studies.
- Key points about critical appraisal and conduct of a review are summarized at the end of each step.

Section A
Steps of a systematic review

This section of the book provides a step-by-step explanation of the processes involved when carrying out a review. There are just five steps. For each step, basic principles of a review are explained, using examples from published reviews. Many examples are followed through the different steps so that readers will be able to see the link between the various stages.

- Step 1: Framing questions for a review

- Step 2: Identifying relevant literature

- Step 3: Assessing the quality of the literature

- Step 4: Summarizing the evidence

- Step 5: Interpreting the findings

Step 1
Framing questions for a review

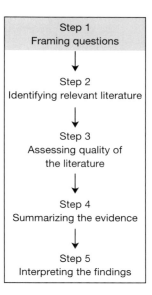

Step 1
Framing questions

↓

Step 2
Identifying relevant literature

↓

Step 3
Assessing quality of
the literature

↓

Step 4
Summarizing the evidence

↓

Step 5
Interpreting the findings

Systematic reviews are carried out to generate answers to focussed questions about health care and related issues. The key to a successful review project lies in the reviewer's ability to be precise and specific when stating the problems to be addressed in the review. This is a critical part of the review because, as will become apparent in subsequent steps, all other aspects of the review flow directly from the original questions. In this step, we will consider the question formulation process in detail and briefly look at the thinking required to examine the potential impact of variations in the different components of a review question.

1.1   An approach to formulating questions

Formulating questions is not as easy as it may sound. A structured approach to framing questions, which uses four components or facets, may by used. These components include the *populations*, *interventions* (or *exposures*), and *outcomes* related to the problem posed in the review, and the *designs* of studies that are suitable for addressing it. We can see the relationship between the various question components in a comparative study in Box 1.1.

After reading Box 1.1 the formulation of questions will probably seem like a daunting task to new reviewers. We may begin to have second thoughts, but we should not give up – help is at hand. This chapter of the book will take us through the question formulation process so that our review can have just the right start. It is well recognized that even quite experienced clinicians don't always find it easy to frame questions for evidence-based practice, so new reviewers can also expect to have a rough ride during the initial stages of their reviews. It will take some effort, but its value will be realized soon, as the rest of the review will flow directly and efficiently from the questions.

Most serious reviewers devote a substantial amount of time and effort in getting the questions right before

Question components
- The *populations*
- The *interventions*
- The *outcomes*
- The *study designs*

Free form question: It describes the query for which you seek an answer through a review in simple language (however vague).

Structured question: Reviewers convert free form questions into a clear and explicit format using a structured approach (see Box 1.2). This makes the query potentially answerable through existing relevant studies.

Box 1.1　Framing structured questions for systematic reviews

Question components

- The populations

  Succinct description of a group of participants or patients, their clinical problem and the healthcare setting.

- The interventions (or exposures)

  The main action(s) being considered, eg treatments, processes of care, social intervention, educational intervention, risk factors, tests, etc.

- The outcomes

  The clinical changes in health state (morbidity, mortality) and other related changes, eg health resource use.

- The study design

  The appropriate ways to recruit participants or patients in a research study, give them interventions and measure their outcomes.

Relationship between the question components in a comparative study

A comparative study assesses the effect of an *intervention* (or *exposure*) using comparison groups. For example, it may allocate participants or patients (with or without randomization) from a relevant *population* to alternative groups of *interventions* (or *exposures*) and follow them up to determine the effect of the *interventions* (or *exposures*) on *outcome*.

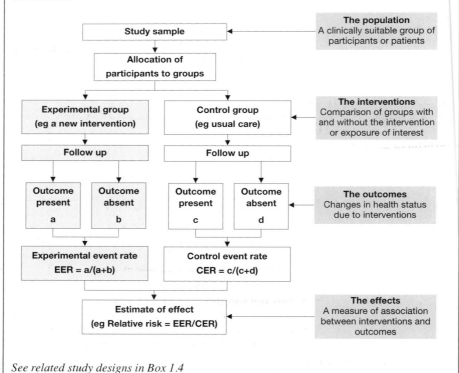

See related study designs in Box 1.4

embarking on a review. They do this because they want to avoid having to change questions later on during the review. We should make no exceptions. If there is any difficulty in figuring out the components of questions, we should first write them down in free form. We can then reconstruct the free form question into a structured format as exemplified in Box 1.2.

We should think of a *population* as a description of the group of participants or patients about whom evidence is being sought in the review. Imagine *interventions* as the actions or the alternatives being considered for the *population*. *Outcomes* are

---

Box 1.2 Some example questions

An example question about clinical effectiveness
Free form question: Which of the many available antimicrobial products improve healing in patients with chronic wounds?
Structured question

• The population	In adults with various forms of chronic wounds in an ambulatory setting ....
• The interventions	.... would systemic or topical antimicrobial preparations ....
• The outcomes	.... improve wound healing?
• The study design	A comparative study that allocates subjects with chronic wounds to alternative therapeutic interventions of interest and determines the effect of the interventions on wound healing (eg randomized controlled trial).

See case study 3 for a related review

An example question about aetiology
Free form question: Is exposure to benzodiazepines in pregnancy associated with malformations in the new-born baby?
Structured question

• The population	In pregnant women. . . .
• The exposures	. . . . does exposure to benzodiazepines during early pregnancy . . . .
• The outcomes	. . . . cause malformations in the new-born baby?
• The study designs	• A study that recruits women in early pregnancy, assesses their exposure to benzodiazepines, follows them up and examines their new-born babies to compare the rates of malformations among women with exposure and those without (cohort study).
	• A study that retrospectively compares exposure to benzodiazepines in early pregnancy among women who have given birth to a child with malformation with that among women who gave birth to a healthy child (case-control study).

See Box 5.2 for a related meta-analysis

continued

LIVERPOOL JOHN MOORES UNIVERSITY
LEARNING SERVICES

Box 1.2   Some example questions (*continued*)

An example question about test accuracy

Free form question: Among postmenopausal women with abnormal vaginal bleeding, does pelvic ultrasound scan exclude uterine cancer accurately?

Structured question

- The population

  In postmenopausal women, within a community setting, with vaginal bleeding....

- The test

  .... does a uterine ultrasound scan test accurately predict ....

- The reference standard

  .... histological diagnosis of uterine cancer?

- The study design

  A study that recruits women from a relevant population, uses the test (scan) and a reference standard investigation to confirm or refute the presence of cancer (histology), and determines the accuracy with which the test identifies cancer (*see Box C4.3*).

See case study 4 for a related review

---

measures of what the *population* wants to achieve from the *interventions*, eg avoiding illness or death. Finally, we should think of how a study could be *designed* to examine the effect of our *interventions*. For example, by comparing *outcomes* between groups of a *population* with and without the *intervention*, the effect may be assessed in terms of illness avoided by use of an *intervention*.

The point about question formulation is that a structured approach should be used. The structure outlined in Box 1.1 should never become a 'straight jacket' and it may be modified to meet the needs of our free form question depending on where our interest in health care lies. For example, in epidemiology the questions may be about aetiology. We can easily substitute the component *interventions* with *exposure* and frame the questions in terms of how *outcomes* might be different in *populations* exposed or not exposed to certain agents or risk factors (Box 1.2). For questions about the accuracy of screening or diagnostic tests we might substitute the component *intervention* with *test*, and *outcome* with *reference standard* against which the accuracy of the *test* will be measured (Box 1.2). In this way the proposed structure is versatile and adaptable for a wide range of question types.

> This book will focus mainly on questions relating to **quantitative** effects of *interventions* (therapy, prevention, social care, etc.) or *exposures* (environmental agents, risk factors, etc.) in the context of **comparative** *study designs*.

1.2   Variations in *populations*, *interventions* and *outcomes*

Once the way in which questions are structured is understood (Box 1.1), we should be able to see that systematic reviews are analyses of existing studies within a given set of *populations*, *interventions* and *outcomes*. We may have started with some scepticism about framing our question in this way; however, with the realization that different *populations*, *interventions* and *outcomes* exist within our free form question, we are likely to end up with many more than one question. If we have not, we should look hard to see if there is some variation within each one of our question components. This is critical – even in a straightforward question about antimicrobials for chronic wounds (Box 1.2), it should be clear that there are many types of chronic wounds (*populations*), antimicrobials (*interventions*) and ways of measuring wound healing (*outcomes*) (Box 1.3).

It is important to seriously consider how *populations*, *interventions* and *outcomes* might vary among existing studies. Such differences are important in defining study selection criteria (Step 2) and planning the tabulation of findings (Step 4). They are also relevant in understanding the reasons for variation in effects of *interventions* from study to study (Step 4) and in exploring the applicability of our findings (Step 5). Thus, conclusions of individual studies and reviews may vary depending on differences in the characteristics of their *populations*, the nature or delivery of their *interventions* and the types of *outcomes*. These issues are examined in detail later on in the book. Here we briefly examine their implications when framing questions.

Population characteristics may vary between studies with respect to patients' age and sex, severity of illness, presence of co-existing illnesses, etc. For instance, when the effect of home visits is studied among elderly people (Box 1.3), the *intervention* is effective among young-old rather than old-old people (Box 4.5). Similarly, the *intervention* features such as the care setting, compliance or intensity, additional routine care, etc. may also be associated with variable effects. For example, among elderly people, home visits are more effective if multidimensional assessments are used and follow-up is frequent (Box 4.5).

We need to identify all clinically relevant and important *outcomes*, which will help in examining the success or failure of our *interventions*. During our review it may become apparent that existing studies have not used *outcomes* we felt were relevant. Identification of these deficiencies in existing studies is important by itself, but sometimes when these data cannot be easily acquired, there may be a tendency to become interested in what are regarded as intermediate, surrogate or proxy *outcomes*. For example, when we are really interested in discovering the effect of fluoride therapy in preventing fractures, we might be tempted to investigate bone mineral content as a surrogate *outcome*, as it would be easier to obtain information about this. How misleading such an approach can be is demonstrated in a randomized controlled trial (*N Engl J Med* 1999; **322**: 802–9); bone density increased significantly (10–35% at different skeletal sites as compared to placebo) among the participants treated with fluorides, however, there was a nearly three-fold increase in non-vertebral fractures (control 24 vs fluorides 72, *p*=0.01), which was unexpected. This example makes it evident that conclusions from research based on surrogate *outcomes* are likely to be less valid for making decisions in practice.

When considering the *outcomes* for a review question, we should think about what we mean by health. Is it just the absence of illness or disease? This book mainly focuses on quantitative morbidity or mortality *outcomes*. It is becoming fashionable to

Box 1.3 Framing questions for reviews: Variations in *population*, *interventions*, *outcomes* and *study designs*

Two example questions about clinical effectiveness

Free form question: Which of the many available antimicrobial products improve healing in patients with chronic wounds?

Structured question *(expanded from Box 1.2)*

• The population	Adults with various forms of chronic wounds:	• Diabetic ulcers • Venous ulcers • Pressure ulcers
• The interventions	Antimicrobial preparations: *versus* Comparator:	• Systemic preparations • Topical preparations *versus* • Other preparations
• The outcomes	Clinical (various measures to quantify improvement in wound healing):	• Complete healing • Wound area remaining • Healing scores
• The study design	Experimental and observational studies: *(see Box 1.4)*	• Randomized controlled trials • Experimental studies without randomization • Cohort studies with concurrent controls

See Case study 3 for a related review

Free form question: Do home visits improve the health of elderly people?

Structured question

• The population	Elderly people in various age groups:	• Young-old • Middle age-old • Old-old
• The interventions	Home visits: *versus* Comparator:	• Intensive assessments • Frequent assessments *versus* • Usual care
• The outcomes	Clinical (various measures to quantify health and health resource use):	• Mortality • Functional status • Nursing home admissions
• The study design	Experimental studies: *(see Box 1.4)*	• Randomized controlled trials • Experimental studies without randomization

See Box 4.5 for a related meta-analysis

An example question about clinical and cost effectiveness

Free form question: To what extent is the risk of post-operative infection reduced by antimicrobial prophylaxis in patients undergoing hip replacement and is it worth the costs?

continued

Box 1.3   Framing questions for reviews: Variations in *population*, *interventions*, *outcomes* and *study designs* (continued)

Structured question

• The population	Patients undergoing hip replacement:	• Various types of procedures
• The interventions	Antimicrobial prophylaxis: *versus*	• Various types of antibiotics *versus*
	Comparator:	• Placebo
		• No antibiotics
• The outcomes	Clinical:	• Post-operative infection
	Economic:	• Cost per infection prevented
• The study design	Clinical:	• Experimental studies (*see Box 1.4*)
	Economic:	• Cost effectiveness analyses

See Box 3.4 for related study quality assessment

---

consider the question of how to achieve optimal clinical *outcomes* with the smallest input of resources. This allows us to discover whether the investment in *interventions* is likely to be worthwhile. In this situation *outcomes* need to focus on the costs of providing health care in addition to clinical *outcomes* (Box 1.3). We will not cover these issues much beyond framing the questions.

1.3   Variations in *study designs*

Let us turn our attention to *study design*, the fourth component of a review question (Box 1.1). For a given set of *populations*, *interventions* and *outcomes*, reviews will provide summaries of existing studies that used different research *designs* (Box 1.2). Why is *design* so important? *Design* of a study determines the validity of the observed effects, ie our confidence that the results of a study are likely to approximate to the 'truth' for the participants or patients studied depends on the soundness of its *design*. In this way *design* serves as a marker of study quality. Its importance cannot be emphasized enough. Ultimately the strength of a review's inferences depends on the integrity of *designs* of the available studies.

Some reviewers consider certain *study designs* to be superior because they feel that the *design* has an inherent value in itself. For example, they may focus exclusively on randomized studies when conducting reviews. Such a view ignores the fact that addressing different types of questions may require the use of different *study designs*. As an example, a question about accuracy of a *test* would require a *study design* that prospectively (without randomization)

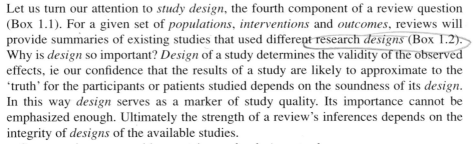

Valid results are said to be unbiased. **Bias** either exaggerates or underestimates the 'true' effect of an *intervention* or *exposure.*

The **quality** of a study depends on the degree to which its design, conduct and analysis minimizes **biases**.

recruits all eligible patients, employs the *test* and the *reference standard* investigation to confirm or refute the presence of disease, and determines the accuracy with which the test correctly identifies disease (case study 4). Assessment of long-term or rare *outcomes*, particularly when examining the safety of *interventions* (as in case study 2), would be more suited for an observational *design*, not an experimental study. For example, cohort and case-control studies, not randomized trials, would evaluate the effect of *exposure* to benzodiazepines in pregnancy on rare malformations in the new-born baby (Box 5.2).

Even for questions concerning effectiveness of *interventions*, where randomized trials are generally preferred, it might be difficult to justify a restriction to using randomized studies only. This may be particularly true when such studies are unethical. Sometimes there is just a dearth of randomized studies. For example, in the review on antimicrobials for chronic wounds (case study 3), despite a comprehensive search, only four clearly randomized studies could be found, so other *designs* had to be included. On the other hand, in case study 2, where the

Effectiveness is the extent to which an *intervention* (therapy, prevention, diagnosis, screening, education, social care, etc.) produces beneficial *outcomes* under ordinary day-to-day circumstances.

review considered safety of water fluoridation, no randomized studies had been published, so it became necessary to consider various other *designs*. Sometimes a review may consider a number of separate but related questions. For example, if a review is to include an assessment of efficiency in addition to effectiveness, then *study designs* for economic evaluation will also be required (Box 1.3). Thus, it might be necessary to consider different *designs* simultaneously in some review questions. This multiplicity of *designs* has implications for study quality assessment (Step 3) and synthesis (Step 4).

Efficiency (cost effectiveness) is the extent to which the balance between input (costs) and output (*outcomes*) of *interventions* represents value for money.

Insistence on randomized studies, ignoring other types of evidence, might paralyse reviewers as such reviews might never find any studies. When faced with having to make decisions for practice, using the best available evidence is likely to be better than not using any evidence at all. We will need to explore the nature of our questions (effectiveness, aetiology, efficiency, accuracy, etc) and the different ways of addressing the specific issues before us, ie *populations*, *interventions* and *outcomes*. Then we should select the *study designs* that are likely to provide the most valid answers and develop a hierarchy of *study designs* suitable for our review. This approach will help us define inclusion and exclusion criteria for selecting studies of a minimum acceptable quality (Step 2).

Each question type has a *design* hierarchy of its own. In this book we focus mainly on questions relating to health effects of *interventions* and *exposures*. These questions usually focus on how one *intervention* or *exposure* compares with another. A hierarchy of *designs* for studies addressing such issues is shown in Box 1.4. The most sound

Box 1.4 A hierarchy of *study designs* for questions about effectiveness of healthcare interventions

Description of the *design*	Levels assigned to evidence based on soundness of *design*[+]

Experimental study
A comparative study* in which the use of different *interventions* among participants is allocated by the researcher.

- **Randomized controlled trial (with concealed allocation)**
  Random allocation of participants to an *intervention* and a control (eg placebo or usual care) group, with follow-up to examine differences in *outcomes* between the two groups. Randomization (with concealment of allocation sequence from caregivers) avoids bias because both known and unknown determinants of outcome, apart from the intervention, are usually equally distributed between the two groups of participants.

  I

- **Experimental study without randomization** (sometimes erroneously called quasi-experimental or quasi-randomized or pseudorandomized studies) A study in which the allocation of participants to different *interventions* is managed by the researcher but the method of allocation falls short of genuine randomization, eg alternate or even–odd allocation. Such methods fail to conceal the allocation sequence from caregivers.

Observational study with control group
A comparative study* in which the use of different *interventions* among participants is not allocated by the researcher (it is merely observed).

II[s]

- **Cohort study**
  Follow-up of participants who receive an *intervention* (that is not allocated by the researcher) to examine the difference in *outcomes* compared to a control group, eg participants receiving no care.
- **Case-control studies**
  Comparison of *intervention* rates between participants with the outcome (cases) and those without the *outcome* (controls).

Observational study without control groups
- **Cross-sectional study**
  Examination of the relationship between *outcomes* and other variables of interest (including interventions) as they exist in a relevant *population* at one particular time.
- **Before-and-after study**
  Comparison of *outcomes* in study participants before and after an *intervention*.
- **Case series**
  Description of a number of cases of an *intervention* and their *outcomes*.

III

Case reports
Pathophysiological studies or bench research
Expert opinion or consensus

IV

---

* *A comparative study assesses the effect of an intervention using comparison groups. See Box 1.1 for an example flow chart of such a study*
[+] *See Box 5.4 for use of levels of evidence in grading recommendations for practice based on reviews of effectiveness*
[s] *In Level II evidence, experimental studies without randomization (and allocation concealment) are considered better than cohort studies, which in turn are considered better than case-control studies*

study design in this context (often called Level I evidence) is one that randomly allocates (concealing the assignment code) participants from a relevant *population* to the alternative *interventions* of interest. This *design* serves to remove selection bias and when conducted well such studies rank at the top of the *study design* hierarchy for effectiveness evidence. Next in the hierarchy are Level II studies where there are three sub-levels. Experimental studies where the allocation of participants or patients is controlled by the researcher, but falls short of genuine randomization and allocation concealment, are considered better than cohort studies, which in turn are considered better than case-control studies. As indicated above, for many reviews experimental studies will not exist (case study 2) or they might be scarce (case study 3). Hence, reviews may have to be conducted using studies of an inferior *design* or using studies with a mixture of *designs*. If our review has several *study designs*, it would be prudent to carefully plan quality assessments (Step 3), stratify study synthesis by *design* and quality (Step 4) and interpret findings cautiously, relying on methodologically sound studies (Step 5).

1.4   Modification of questions during a review

It is important that review questions are formulated *a priori*, that is before the review work is actually commenced. Otherwise the review process may be unduly driven by presuming particular findings. In order to get the questions correct at the beginning, it may be worth involving experienced reviewers and practitioners in the process. This is just one of several reasons why it is considered unwise to prepare a review alone.

Questions will initially be developed without detailed knowledge of much of the relevant literature. Therefore, we should not be surprised if it becomes evident during the review that some questions need to be modified in light of the accumulated research. The commandment 'thou shall pose questions for a review *a priori*' should not be applied too rigidly. We should allow exploration of unexpected issues in the review process; as a greater understanding of the problem is developed during the course of the review, it would be foolish not to do so. If the ongoing work identifies a need for answering questions that had not been foreseen, it would be quite reasonable to raise new questions or to modify existing questions. Such modifications are justifiable if they are based on the realization of alternative ways of defining the *populations*, *interventions*, *outcomes* or *study designs*, which were not considered earlier.

Revision of questions will inevitably have some implications for the review work. The protocol would have to be revised. Literature searches (Step 2), which are usually conducted before questions are refined, may also need refinement and they might have to be run again in the light of the changes to the questions. Study selection criteria will have to be altered. For example, in the review of safety of water fluoridation in case study 2, the original questions were modified in the light of information gathered about the extent and range of quality of available evidence during the initial part of the review. This led to changes in study selection criteria, which are provided in detail in the published report of the review (www.york.ac.uk/inst/crd/fluorid.pdf). Reviewers should not be economical with the truth about question formulation and refinement. It is helpful to be explicit about the modifications and indicate which questions were posed *a priori* and which were generated during the review work. *important to say*

Summary of Step 1: Framing questions for a review

Key points about appraising review articles

- Examine the abstract and the introduction to see if the review is based on predefined questions.
- Examine the methods and other sections to check if questions were modified during the review process.
- Can we be sure that the questions have not been unduly influenced by the knowledge of results of the studies?

Key points about conducting reviews

- The problems to be addressed by the review should be specified in the form of clear, unambiguous questions before beginning the review work.
- Questions should be structured, eg in terms of *population*, *interventions*, *outcomes* and *study designs* relevant to the healthcare issues being addressed in the review.
- Characteristics of the *populations*, differences in *interventions*, variation in *outcomes* and variety in *study designs* may influence the results of a review. The impact of these factors should be carefully considered at this stage.
- Once the review questions have been set, modifications to the protocol should only be allowed after careful consideration. Sometimes, alternative ways of defining the *populations*, *interventions*, *outcomes* or *study designs* become apparent after commencing the review. In this situation it would be reasonable to alter the original questions, but these modifications should not be driven by the knowledge of results of the studies.

Step 2
Identifying relevant literature

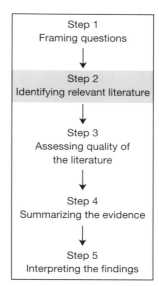

Step 1
Framing questions

Step 2
Identifying relevant literature

Step 3
Assessing quality of
the literature

Step 4
Summarizing the evidence

Step 5
Interpreting the findings

Being thorough when identifying the relevant literature is a crucial condition for a systematic review. It is driven by the desire to capture as many relevant studies as possible. In published reviews, literature searches are often summarized too simplistically to allow others to replicate them. A good search can vary between simple and relatively complex depending on the review topic. Not all searches are beyond the reach of novice reviewers.

A comprehensive literature search includes multistage and iterative processes. First we will need to generate lists of citations from relevant resources (eg electronic bibliographic databases, reference lists of known primary and review articles, and relevant journals). Second, we will need to screen these citations for relevance to our review questions with a view to obtaining the full manuscripts of all potentially relevant studies. Third, we will need to sift through these manuscripts to make the final inclusion/exclusion decisions based on explicit study selection criteria. Some of the studies will provide reference lists from which we will find more potentially relevant citations, and the cycle of obtaining manuscripts and examining them for relevance will go one more round. These processes will eventually lead to a set of studies on which the review will be based. In the report of our review, a flowchart of the study identification process will be required (Box 2.1). The basic principles behind the identification of relevant literature covering various aspects of this flowchart are covered in this step.

Precision of effect in a review refers to its uncertainty. Poor searches may contribute to uncertainty by identifying only a fraction of the available studies, which leads to wide confidence intervals around the summary effects. Imprecision refers to uncertainty arising due to play of chance, but not due to **bias**.

2.1 Generating a list of potentially relevant citations

The precision and validity of the findings of reviews are directly related to the comprehensiveness of the literature identification process. The aim of the initial searches, both electronic and manual, is to generate as comprehensive a list of citations as possible to address the questions being posed in the review. Thus, the search strategy (search terms and the resources to be searched) will depend on the components of the questions. If we have formulated the questions well, we have already made a head start. In practical terms, developing a search strategy may take

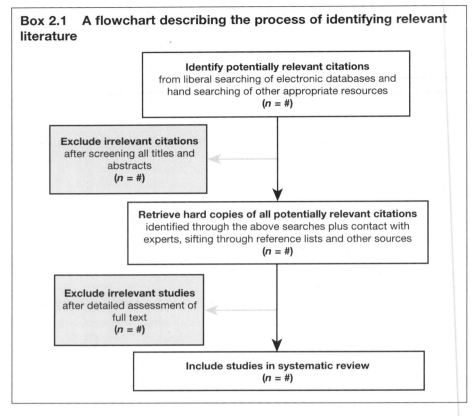

Box 2.1 A flowchart describing the process of identifying relevant literature

Identify potentially relevant citations
from liberal searching of electronic databases and hand searching of other appropriate resources
(n = #)

Exclude irrelevant citations
after screening all titles and abstracts
(n = #)

Retrieve hard copies of all potentially relevant citations
identified through the above searches plus contact with experts, sifting through reference lists and other sources
(n = #)

Exclude irrelevant studies
after detailed assessment of full text
(n = #)

Include studies in systematic review
(n = #)

Validity of a review refers to the methods used to minimize **bias**. **Bias** will either exaggerate or underestimate the 'true' effect being sought in a review. Poor searches contribute to **bias** as they may preferentially identify studies with particularly positive or particularly negative effects.

several iterations, so we should be prepared for the hard work. However, using a systematic approach (similar to the one outlined below) can quickly lead us to a reasonably effective strategy.

The steps involved in electronically generating lists of potentially relevant citations include selection of relevant databases, formulation of an appropriate combination of search terms and retrieval of citations from the searches. Searches undertaken at the beginning of the review may have to be updated at a later date depending on the length of time taken to complete the review.

2.1.1   Selection of relevant databases to search

There exists no such database that covers all publications from all healthcare journals. Serious reviewers usually search many databases. How should we decide about database coverage? This depends very much on the topic of the review. Why not compare and contrast the types of databases searched in Case study 2 (Box C2.1) with those searched in Case study 3

(Box C3.1): the differences are mainly due to differences in the nature of the review topics. There are many useful databases and we may wish to ask our local librarian or consult one of the guides to databases. Some of the commonly used databases are shown in Box 2.2.

Box 2.2 Important databases of research in health care

Selected general databases
- **MEDLINE** (available freely via PubMed at www.ncbi.nlm.nih.gov/PubMed)
  Bibliographic records (with and without abstracts) of biomedical literature from 1966 onwards.
- **EMBASE** (www.embase.com)
  Records of biomedical literature from 1974 onwards.
- **Science Citation Index** (www.isinet.com/isi/products/citation/sci)
  Relevant studies found through electronic or manual searches can be used to identify further relevant citations by electronically locating other citations on the same topic through citation search on Science Citation Index.

Selected databases with a specific focus
- **PsycInfo**
  Records of literature on psychology and related behavioural and social sciences from 1987.
- **CENTRAL** (The Cochrane Central Register of Controlled Trials)
  Records of clinical trials in health care identified through the work of the Cochrane Collaboration, including large numbers of citations from MEDLINE and EMBASE as well as citations not covered by these databases. In the 4th issue of the 2002 Cochrane Library there were 345 378 trials in CENTRAL.
- **CINAHL** (Cumulative Index to Nursing and Allied Health Literature)
  Records of literature on all aspects of nursing and allied health disciplines.
- **NHS EED** (NHS Economic Evaluation Database)
  Structured abstracts of economic evaluations of healthcare interventions identified by regular searching of bibliographic databases and hand searching of key major medical journals.
- **MIDIRS** (www.midirs.org)
  A broad reference resource available to obstetricians, midwives and consumers.
- **Conference Papers Index**
  Records of conference presentations.
- **Research Registers** (for research in progress)
  Guide to selected registers – www.york.ac.uk/inst/crd/htadbase.htm
  National Research Register (NRR) – www.doh.gov.uk/research/nrr.htm
  MetaRegister of Current Controlled Trials – http://controlled-trials.com
  www.nci.nih.gov/clinical_trials
- **SIGLE** (System for Information on Grey Literature – http://stneasy.fiz-karlsruhe.de)
  Bibliographic database covering European non-conventional (so-called grey) literature in the field of pure and applied natural sciences and other areas.

See Box C2.1 and C3.2 for some other databases searched in the case studies

---

Most reviews would include searches in general databases such as MEDLINE and EMBASE, which cover many of the same journals. MEDLINE is produced by the US National Library of Medicine and has a North American emphasis. EMBASE has a greater European emphasis in terms of the journals it covers and has a high pharmacological content. Local medical libraries or professional bodies may provide free access to both MEDLINE and EMBASE – for example, the British Medical Association provides access to its members (see www.ovid.bma.org.uk). To complicate matters, there are a number of different commercial software interfaces for electronic databases, eg Ovid, Silverplatter, Knowledgefinder, etc. Their mode of searching is flexible and user-friendly, but they are more costly than the PubMed interface to MEDLINE which is freely available on the Internet. The PubMed interface has an additional searching feature via its 'Related Articles' function, which allows capture of additional citations on the basis of their similarity to known relevant citations.

2.1.2 Search term combination for electronic database searches

MeSH or Medical Subject Headings are controlled terms used in the MEDLINE database to index citations. Other bibliographic databases use MeSH-like terms.

In simple terms, building a suitable combination of search terms involves combining free text words and controlled terms (MeSH or MeSH-like terms) which represent the various components of the review question.

We should begin by examining the *populations*, *interventions*, *outcomes* and *study designs* relevant to our review, as shown in Box 2.3. For each one of these components we will need to compile a list of words that authors might have used in their studies. We may identify a range of synonyms with spelling variations by examining the relevant studies we already know of. These will provide the free text words for our search. We will also need to compile a list of controlled terms that database indexers might have used when recording the citations. There are many ways to identify relevant MeSH or MeSH-like terms. For example, we may look at the key words suggested for indexing in known relevant studies (frequently found at the end of the abstract) and check how they are actually indexed in the databases we want to search. We need to keep in mind that indexers don't always follow authors' suggestions. Each database has its own thesaurus or index structure and we may want to refer to this for additional MeSH terms. This task is made easier in databases that offer the opportunity to map free text words we have selected to MeSH in their index lists. However we select our search terms, we must ensure that an adequate number of free text words and controlled terms are included to represent each component of the question. This will enhance the sensitivity of our search, increasing our ability to capture a large proportion of the relevant studies.

Sensitivity of a search is the proportion of relevant studies identified by a search strategy expressed as a percentage of all relevant studies on a given topic. It is a measure of the comprehensiveness of a search method. Do not confuse with sensitivity of a test.

The next stage is to combine the words and terms we have selected to capture the various components of the question.

Box 2.3   How to develop a search term combination for searching electronic bibliographic databases

An example of a search term combination for Ovid MEDLINE database

Free form question: In women undergoing surgical termination of pregnancy, does antibiotic prophylaxis reduce the risk of post-operative infection?

Structured question (not all components may be needed for searching)

- The population   Pregnant women undergoing surgical abortion
- The interventions   Antibiotics used as prophylaxis
                       Comparator: placebo or no intervention (not used in search term combination)
- The outcome   Post-operative infection
- The study design   Experimental studies (not used in search term combination)

Question components and relevant search terms	Type of terms		Boolean operator
	Free	MeSH	(*see glossary*)
The population: Pregnant women undergoing surgical abortion			
1 (terminat$ adj3 pregnan$).tw	x		
2 (unwant$ adj3 pregnan$).tw	x		
3 abortion$.tw	x		OR (captures
4 exp abortion induced/		x	*population*)
5 exp pregnancy unwanted/		x	
6 or/1-5			
The interventions: Antibiotics used as prophylaxis			
7 exp infection control/		x	
8 exp anti-infective agents/		x	
9 exp antibiotics/		x	OR (captures
10 antibiotic$.tw	x		*interventions*)
11 (antibiotic adj3 prophyla$).tw	x		
12 (antimicrobial$ or anti-microbial$).tw	x		
13 or/7-12			
The outcome: Post-operative infection			
14 exp bacterial infections/		x	
15 exp postoperative complications/		x	
16 sepsis/		x	
17 exp abortion septic/		x	
18 exp endometritis/		x	
19 exp adnexitis/		x	
20 (postoperative adj3 (infect$ or contaminat$ or complicat$ or pyrexi$)).tw	x		OR (captures
21 (sepsis or septic).tw	x		*outcome*)
22 (bacteria$ adj3 (contaminat$ or infect$)).tw	x		
23 (post-abort$ adj3 (infect$ or complicat$ or contaminat$)).tw	x		
24 endometritis.tw	x		
25 pelvic inflammatory disease.tw	x		
26 (septic adj3 abort$).tw	x		
27 or/14-26			
28 and/6,13,27			AND (combines all components)

continued

Box 2.3   How to develop a search term combination for searching electronic bibliographic databases (*continued*)

Commands and symbols for Ovid MEDLINE

$	Truncation, eg pregnan$ will pick up pregnant, pregnancy and pregnancies
adj	Proximity and adjacency searching, eg terminat$ adj pregnan$ means that these terms appear next to each other, terminat$ adj3 pregnan$ means that there may be three other words in between them
.tw	Textword search, eg abortion$.tw will search for textwords in title or abstract
/	Medical subject heading (MeSH) search, eg abortion induced/ will search for MeSH in indexing terms
exp	Explodes the MeSH, eg exp abortion induced/ will search for this MeSH as well as the lower order MeSH terms included under the MeSH abortion induced in tree structure such as abortion eugenic, abortion legal, abortion therapeutic, pregnancy reduction multifetal

See related selection criteria in Box 2.5
Based on RCOG Clinical Governance Advice No. 3 (www.rcog.org.uk/mainpages.asp?PageID=318)

Boolean logic refers to the logical relationship among search terms.

Boolean operators AND, OR and NOT are used during literature searches to include or exclude certain citations from electronic databases. An example of their use in PubMed is shown below:

Coke / Cola
547 + 5 + 406 / PubMed
Citations
Coke = **552**
Cola = **411**
Coke **AND** Cola = **5**
Coke **OR** Cola = **958**
Coke **NOT** Cola = **547**
Cola **NOT** Coke = **406**

This is achieved by Boolean logic, which commonly uses the operators AND, OR and NOT to create sets of citations from the search terms. For example, combining *coke* OR *cola* will retrieve all citations where either one or both of these terms are found. On the other hand, combining *coke* AND *cola* will only retrieve citations where both of these terms are found. Combining *coke* NOT *cola* will retrieve citations that contain the term *coke* only, thereby excluding all citations with the term *cola*. Needless to say that NOT should be used with great caution. In general, one would use OR to combine all the words and terms capturing a component of the question. This will give a large citation set for each component that we searched for. We can now combine these with AND to produce a set which contains citations relevant to all the various components of the question.

Box 2.3 only shows the search term combinations for the MEDLINE database. Any search term combinations developed for MEDLINE would need to be adapted to the peculiarities of each one of the other databases to be searched. This usually requires professional support. It can be guaranteed that this will not be easy, particularly because different databases use different terms and index structures. But we should not lose sight of our objective, which is to produce a valid answer for the questions raised for the review. There is substantial evidence that limiting the search to only a few databases tends to bias the review. The more broad based our search, the more likely it is that our review will produce a precise and valid answer.

2.1.3 Searching for study designs

One important component of the review question is *study design*, which can be used to improve our search strategy. For example, to identify published and unpublished clinical trials we may search specialist collections such as the Cochrane Central Register of Controlled Trials (CENTRAL) and research registers of ongoing trials (http://controlled-trials.com). These are usually the first databases to be searched in reviews of randomized studies. However, for other *study designs* such collections are rare.

General databases have subject indexing for some *study designs* but this alone may not be adequate for searching. Therefore search term combinations which capture studies of a particular *design* (also known as search filters) have been developed by information specialists. It is tempting to search general databases using such *design* filters, eg those available on PubMed Clinical Queries (www.ncbi.nlm.nih.gov/entrez/query/static/clinical.html) or on health technology assessment websites, for example www.york.ac.uk/inst/crd/search.htm. Some filters are designed to perform quick searches to support day-to-day evidence-based practice. They will make our search more precise but inevitably this will be at the expense of sensitivity. This means that a high proportion of citations retrieved by filtered searches will be relevant, but many relevant citations will be missed because they are not indexed in a way that the filter can pick up. This is a major drawback because systematic reviews should be based on searches that are as thorough as possible. There is one exception – for reviews of randomized trials where indexing of *design*-related terms is more reasonable, carefully adapted versions of existing filters for therapy questions may be used (see case study 3).

> **Precision of a search** is the proportion of relevant studies identified by a search strategy. This is expressed as a percentage of all studies (relevant and irrelevant) identified by that strategy. It is a measure of the ability of a search to exclude irrelevant studies. Do not confuse with precision of effect.

2.1.4 Reference lists and other sources (eg journals, grey literature, conference proceedings)

Inaccurate or incomplete indexing of articles and journals in electronic bibliographic databases requires the examination of other sources of citations. Reference lists from identified studies and related reviews provide a rich source of potentially relevant citations. Index Medicus and Excerpta Medica can be manually searched if it is desirable to identify studies prior to the start dates of the electronic databases (as in case study 2). The latest issues of the key journals may also be searched to identify very recent studies which have not yet been included on the electronic databases or cited by others. It can take more than a year for studies published in some journals indexed in MEDLINE to finally appear in this database.

Many studies published in technical reports, discussion papers or other formats are not included in major databases and journals, but some of these may be indexed on databases such as SIGLE (System for Information on Grey Literature), the National Technical Information Service (www.ntis.gov/search.htm), and the British National Bibliography for Report Literature (www.bl.uk/) etc. The libraries of specialist research organizations and professional societies may provide another useful source of this grey literature. Dissertations and theses can also be routes into obtaining otherwise unpublished research and these are recorded in databases such as Dissertation Abstracts and CINAHL (Cumulative Index to Nursing and Allied Health Literature). Conference proceedings can provide information on research in progress as well as completed research. We can access this information through the Index of Scientific and Technical Proceedings (http://wos.mimas.ac.uk/), the Conference Papers Index and in the catalogues of large research libraries.

2.1.5   Identifying ongoing research

Bias in study retrieval can either exaggerate or underestimate the 'true' effect of an *intervention* or *exposure* in a review.

The most unbiased study retrieval can only be guaranteed in those few areas where prospective comprehensive research registers are maintained. These research registers may provide information on completed or ongoing studies. Box 2.2 shows some electronic resources to search for ongoing studies. Many pharmaceutical companies hold their study results in private databases, which may occasionally be released on request (as in case study 1).

2.1.6   Searching the Internet

This is how most research will be published and accessed in the future. Many of the electronic databases described above are available through the Internet. The 'world wide web' can also be used to identify researchers and manufacturers as well as completed and ongoing studies. Given the enormity of the web, any serious attempt to search it would be a major undertaking, with tens of thousands of web pages to browse. A structured approach would have to be developed, for example using meta-search engines (eg Copernic – www.copernic.com, Dogpile – www.dogpile.com, Google – www.google.com, etc.), or search engines with a healthcare focus (eg Turning Research Into Practice – www.tripdatabase.com/, Organising Medical Networked Information – www.omni.ac.uk, MedNets – www.mednets.com/ smedlink.htm, etc.). For systematic reviews of healthcare literature, the value of the contribution made by searching the Internet is unknown, but is likely to be limited at the time of writing this book. The web technology is changing and improving rapidly. Internet searching, which can be difficult and possibly inefficient at this time, might become easier and more efficient in the near future.

2.1.7   Seeking professional input

After reading through this section we might feel that literature identification is beyond your current searching skills and may feel the need for professional input. Many professional reviewers receive support from information specialists to carry out their searches. Our local librarian may be able to help – they might be able to direct us to an information service that conducts systematic literature searches. Registering our review with a relevant Review Group of the Cochrane Collaboration might allow us access to professional searches. Many of the Review Groups have developed comprehensive search strategies in their topics and maintain specialized registers.

(Import) &

2.2 Citation retrieval and management

In order to effectively manage the process of literature identification, citations obtained from the searches will have to be imported into a computer program for reference management (eg Reference Manager, ProCite, EndNote). Construction of a master citation database for a review will involve collating all the citations from various sources. Built-in functions of the citation management software allow exact and inexact duplicates (where titles, authors or journal names of the same articles are cited or stated in different manners) to be easily detected. Additional functions of the software can add labels or tags to the citations, by creation of user-defined fields, allowing for enhanced sorting and documentation of the selection process. Searches of some of the sources (eg CENTRAL) may not be importable directly into the master citation database. Citations from these sources will have to be scrutinized and managed using simple word-processing software. In addition, searches of non-electronic sources (eg reference lists of known articles) may be managed manually. Eventually many citations will have to be manually entered into the master citation database of the review.

> The **Cochrane Collaboration** is an international collaboration that aims to help with informed decision-making on healthcare topics by preparing, maintaining and ensuring accessibility of systematic reviews of interventions (www.cochrane.org).

Important to say I think

2.3 Selecting relevant studies ✗

The aim of the study selection process is to use the citation lists to identify those articles that definitely address the questions being posed in the review. This is part of the multi-stage process described in Box 2.1. The process consists of defining the study selection criteria, screening the citations to obtain the full reports of all studies that are likely to meet the selection criteria, and sifting through these manuscripts to make the final inclusion/exclusion decisions.

> **Selecting relevant citations**
> - Develop selection criteria
> - Select relevant citations
> - Obtain full papers and select those relevant
> - Do not use language restrictions

2.3.1 Study selection criteria

These should follow on logically from the review question. Box 2.4 shows example sets of selection criteria defined in terms of the *populations*, *interventions*, *outcome*, and *study designs* of interest. Ultimately, only studies that meet all of the inclusion criteria (and none of the exclusion criteria) will be included in the review. To avoid bias in the selection process, the criteria (both inclusion and exclusion) should be defined *a priori*.

LIVERPOOL
JOHN MOORES UNIVERSITY
AVRIL ROBARTS LRC
TITHEBARN STREET
LIVERPOOL L2 2ER
TEL. 0151 231 4022

Box 2.4   Some examples of study selection criteria

Free form question: In women undergoing surgical termination of pregnancy, does antibiotic prophylaxis reduce the risk of post-operative infection? (*see structured question in Box 2.3*)

Question component	*Inclusion criteria*	*Exclusion criteria*
• The population	Pregnant women undergoing surgical abortion	Other operations
• The interventions	Antibiotics compared to placebo or no prophylaxis; comparison of different antibiotics	Lack of comparison
• The outcome	Post-operative infection confirmed by appropriate microbiological techniques	Infection not confirmed
• The study design	Experimental studies	Observational studies

Free form question: Is it safe to provide population-wide drinking water fluoridation to prevent caries?

Questions component	*Inclusion criteria*	*Exclusion criteria*
• The populations	Populations receiving drinking water sourced through a public water supply	Unsourced water supply
• The interventions	Fluoridation of drinking water, naturally occurring or artificially added, compared to non-fluoridated water	Lack of comparison
• The outcome	Cancer, bone fractures and fluorosis	Outcomes not related to safety
• The study design	– Experimental studies – Observational studies (cohort, case-control, cross-sectional, and before-and-after)	– Case series – Case reports

See case study 2 for a related review

Free form question: Which of the many available antimicrobial products improve healing in patients with chronic wounds? (*see structured question in Box 1.3*)

Question component	*Inclusion criteria*	*Exclusion criteria*
• The populations	Adults with chronic wounds	Other wounds
• The interventions	Systemic and topical antimicrobial preparations compared to placebo or no antimicrobial; comparison of different antibiotics	Lack of comparison
• The outcome	Wound healing	Wound healing not assessed
• The study design	– Randomized controlled trials – Experimental studies without randomization – Cohort studies with concurrent controls	– Studies with historical controls – Case control studies

See case study 3 for a related review

See Box 1.4 for a brief description of various study designs

When defining selection criteria, we should ask ourselves:

- Is it sensible to group various *populations* together?
- Is it sensible to combine various *interventions* together?
- What *outcomes* are clinically relevant?
- What *study designs* should be included/excluded?

Often reviewers are led by what is likely to be reported rather than by what is clinically important, but it is preferable to select studies with clinically important rather than surrogate *outcomes* (Step 1). Whatever decision is taken about study selection will have consequences for the rest of the review. It is up to us as the reviewers to decide on how broad or narrow the selection criteria should be. Criteria that are too broadly defined may make it difficult to synthesize studies; criteria that are too narrowly defined may reduce the applicability of the findings of our review. A balanced approach can enhance the applicability of our findings. For example, using liberal inclusion criteria concerning the *populations* may allow investigation of questions concerning the variation in effects among different *population* subgroups (see Box 4.5).

Ideally studies of the most robust *design* should be included. However, practically, the criteria concerning *study design* may be influenced by knowing the type and amount of available literature to some extent (after initiating the review). If the selection criteria are modified in the light of the information gathered from the initial searches, the modifications should be justified and explicitly reported. When studies of robust *designs* have not been carried out (case study 2) or if they are scarce (case study 3), the inclusion criterion specifying the *study design* may have to consider studies of methodologically poorer quality. This approach may be used in reviews where the goal is to summarize the currently available evidence for decision making, as in case studies 2 and 3. If a review has several *study designs*, it would have implications on study quality assessments (Step 3), study synthesis (Step 4) and interpretation of findings (which should be cautious, based mainly on methodologically superior studies) (Step 5).

2.3.2 Screening of citations  *Important*

Initially, the selection criteria should be applied liberally to the citation lists generated from searching relevant literature sources. Citations often contain only limited information, so any titles (and abstracts) which seem potentially relevant should provisionally be included for consideration on the basis of the full text articles. However, many citations will clearly be irrelevant and these can be excluded at this stage. Two reviewers should carry out citation screening independently and the full manuscripts of all citations considered relevant by any of the reviewers should be obtained. The yield of this process will vary from one review to another.

2.3.3 Obtaining full manuscripts

From a visit to our nearest medical library we will be able to find out the lists and dates of journals that we can obtain locally. However, first it is worth checking on the

Internet for freely available journals (www.freemedicaljournals.com) and then download the papers electronically. Your institution or library may also subscribe to electronic journals not freely available. In this way, many recent publications may be quickly obtained. The next step will be to obtain articles not available through our library or on the Internet. This could be time consuming and help from the local librarian or from a librarian at a professional body will be invaluable. On occasion it may be necessary to write to the authors directly to obtain the papers.

2.3.4 Study selection

The final inclusion/exclusion decisions should be made after examining the full texts of all the potentially relevant citations. We should carefully assess the information contained in these to see whether the criteria have been met or not. Many of the doubtful citations initially included may be confidently excluded at this stage. It will be useful to construct a list of excluded studies at this point, detailing the reason for each exclusion. This will not take much time and providing this list as part of our review increases the quality of our report. When submitting a manuscript of a review for publication in a printed journal, it may not be possible to include this section due to restrictions on space. However, these details can be provided in an electronic version of the journal or they could be made available from our offices on request.

Two independent reviewers should undertake assessments of citations and manuscripts for selection because even when explicit inclusion criteria are prespecified, the decisions concerning inclusion/exclusion can be relatively subjective. For example, when applying the *study design* criteria for selection, reviewers may disagree about including or excluding a study due to unclear reporting. The selection criteria can initially be piloted in a subset of studies where duplicate assessments allow reviewers to gauge whether they can be applied in a constant fashion. If the agreement between the reviewers is poor in the pilot phase, revision of the selection criteria may be required. Once these issues have been clarified, any subsequent disagreements are usually simple oversights, which are easily resolved by consensus. Occasionally arbitration by a third reviewer may be required. Beware of reviews that have only one author; it is likely that errors will have been made in selecting studies.

2.3.5 Selecting studies with duplicate publication

Reviewers often encounter multiple publications of the same study. Sometimes these will be exact duplications, but at other times they might be serial publications with the more recent papers reporting increasing numbers of participants or lengths of follow-up. Inclusion of duplicated data would inevitably bias the data synthesis in the review, particularly because studies with more positive results are more likely to be duplicated. However, the examination of multiple reports of the same study may provide useful information about its quality and other characteristics not captured by a single report. Therefore, all such reports should be examined. However, the data should only be counted once using the largest, most complete report with the longest follow up.

2.4   Publication and related biases

Identification of all the relevant studies depends on their accessibility. Some studies may be less accessible due to:

> **Publication bias** is said to arise when the likelihood of publication of studies, and thus their accessibility to reviewers, is related to the significance of their results regardless of their quality.

- a lack of statistical significance in their results
- the type and language of their reports
- the timing of their publication
- their indexing in databases.

Studies in which *interventions* are not found to be effective, are less likely to be published or they are published in less accessible formats. Publication bias may also involve studies that report certain positive effects that go against strong prevailing beliefs. Systematic reviews that fail to identify such studies will inevitably exaggerate or underestimate the effect of an *intervention* and this is when publication bias arises. Thus the use of a systematic approach to track down less accessible studies is crucial for avoiding bias in systematic reviews. Hopefully in the future, with prospective registration of primary studies, there will be less concern about overlooking studies. Until this happens, it will be necessary to search hard to protect reviews against publication bias. In Step 5 we see how the risk of publication and related biases can be investigated in a review using a funnel plot analysis (Box 5.1).

2.4.1   Searching multiple databases

There is evidence that limiting the search to only a few databases tends to bias the review. We need to cast as wide a net as possible to capture as many citations as possible. Case studies 2 and 3 demonstrate the great lengths serious reviewers can go to when searching for citations. Similarly, if our review is to be taken seriously, we will have to search multiple (overlapping) sources of citations.

2.4.2   Language restrictions in study selection

There is no good reason for excluding articles published in languages that we cannot read or understand. There is increasing evidence that studies with positive findings are more likely to be published in English language journals. Studies with negative findings from non-English speaking countries are frequently published in local language journals. Therefore positive studies are more likely to be accessed if searches are limited to English language, thereby introducing bias. In addition, language restrictions may decrease the precision of the summary effect in our meta-analysis. For these reasons it may be helpful to find some interpretation facilities. If our review is registered with a relevant Cochrane Review Group, there might be help available for dealing with foreign language papers. Otherwise we may have to tackle this issue by obtaining access to translation facilities or by asking other people to extract the necessary data for us. Sorry, but there is no easy way out.

Summary of Step 2: Identifying relevant literature

Key points about appraising review articles

- Examine the methods section to see if the searches appear to be comprehensive:
  - check if search term combinations follow from the question
  - list the resources (eg databases) searched to identify primary studies
  - have any relevant resources been left out?
  - were any restrictions applied by dates, language, etc?
- Were the selection criteria set *a priori*? How reliably were they applied?
- Have analyses been conducted to examine for the risk of publication and related biases? (Step 5)
- How likely is it that relevant studies might have been missed? And what is the potential impact on the conclusions of the review?

Key points about conducting reviews

- The search for studies should be extensive and the selection process should minimize bias.
- The search term combination should follow from the question and it should be designed to cast a wide net for capturing as many potentially relevant citations as possible. Multiple resources (both computerized and printed) should be searched. Searches undertaken at the beginning may have to be updated towards the end of the review depending on the length of time taken to review.
- A systematic approach to citation management should be used to manage the review efficiently.
- Study selection criteria should flow directly from the review questions; they should be set *a priori* and should be piloted to check that they can be reliably applied.
- When sifting through the citations, selection criteria should be applied liberally to retrieve full manuscripts of all potentially relevant citations.
- Final inclusion/exclusion decisions should be made after examination of the full manuscripts. Reasons for inclusion and exclusion should be recorded.
- Language restriction should not be applied in searching or in study selection.
- Duplicate independent assessments of citations and manuscripts should be performed to reduce the risk of errors of judgement in the study selection.
- If feasible, an analysis should be undertaken to explore for the risk of publication and related biases (Step 5).

Step 3

Assessing the quality of the literature

It cannot be emphasized enough that the quality of the studies included in a systematic review is the 'Achilles heel' behind its conclusions. Therefore we should consider study quality at every step in a review. The quality of a study may be defined as the degree to which it employs measures to minimize bias and error in its *design*, conduct and analysis. We have briefly considered the importance of *study design* as a general marker of study quality when framing questions (Step 1) and selecting studies (Step 2). This approach helps to crudely define the weakest acceptable *study design*, thereby excluding studies with lower levels of quality.

Once studies of a minimum acceptable quality (based on *design*) have been selected, an in-depth critical appraisal will allow us to assess the quality of the evidence in a more refined way. Step 3 explains how to develop and use checklists for detailed assessments of selected studies for their quality. These refined and detailed quality assessments will be used later in evidence synthesis (Step 4) and interpretation (Step 5). In this way, the checklists will help judge the strength of a review's inferences. In this step we will focus on quality assessment of studies on effectiveness of *interventions*. Details of quality assessment of studies on safety of *interventions* and accuracy of tests can be found in case studies 2 and 4 respectively.

3.1 Development of quality assessment checklists

Quality assessment will usually be based on an appraisal of individual aspects of a study's *design*, conduct and analysis (often called quality items) – evidence of deficiencies may raise the possibility of bias. We can find quality items in one of the many published guides on critical appraisal of healthcare literature (see users' guides to evidence-based practice at www.cche.net/usersguides/main.asp). These guides are usually written for supporting evidence-based practice and provide advice on appraisal of individual studies according to the nature of the clinical query, which we

Step 1
Framing questions
↓
Step 2
Identifying relevant literature
↓
Step 3
Assessing quality of the literature
↓
Step 4
Summarizing the evidence
↓
Step 5
Interpreting the findings

3

Bias either exaggerates or underestimates the 'true' effect of an *intervention* or *exposure*.

Systematic error (or **bias**) leads effects to depart systematically, either lower or higher, from the 'true' effect.

Random error is due to the play of chance and leads effects to be imprecise (wide confidence intervals).

Box 3.1   Study quality assessment in a systematic review

1) Define the question and the selection criteria:
- Consider the nature of the questions being posed
- Consider the types of relevant *study designs*
- Determine a quality threshold (*study design* threshold) which defines the weakest acceptable *design* for selection (Step 2)

2) Develop or select a quality checklist
Identify a suitable existing checklist for your review topic. If one does not exist, develop a new quality checklist considering relevant quality items grouped as follows:
- Generic items related to relevant *study designs* depending on the nature of the review question (usually obtained from published critical appraisal guides or existing quality checklists)
- Specific items related to the *populations*, *interventions* and *outcomes* of the review question

3) Examine the reliability of checklist use:
- Assess the reliability of the checklist in a pilot phase before applying it to all the selected studies

4) Incorporate the quality assessments into the systematic review
We may use the quality assessment for all or some of the following:
- To describe the quality of studies included in a review
- To explore quality differences as an explanation for the variation in effects from study to study (Step 4)
- To make decisions regarding pooling the effects observed in included studies (Step 4)
- To aid in determining the strength of inferences (Step 5)
- To make recommendations about how future studies could be performed better

---

delineate when framing our question (Step 1). The items in these guides can be used as a basis for developing a checklist to perform an in-depth appraisal of the quality of each study included in a review.

There are many published quality assessment checklists for use in systematic reviews; but beware, most have not been developed with scientific rigour. A whole range of quality items is emphasized in the various checklists but some items may not be related to bias. By assigning numerical values to items, some checklists create a scale in an attempt to provide an overall quantitative quality score for each study. Many checklists neatly classify studies into low or high quality subgroups based on their compliance with the quality items. If we took a leap of faith and randomly selected one of these published quality checklists for our review, we might find ourselves in trouble. On closer examination we might find that not all items in the checklist were relevant to our review, and some relevant items were not part of the checklist. For instance, blind *outcome* assessment is emphasized in most checklists. Blinding might be of marginal importance for an unambiguous *outcome* such as mortality, but it is fundamental in the assessment of subjective *outcomes* such as pain. The numerical values assigned to the items for scoring quality may not be suitable for every review; the same is true of the arbitrariness in the criteria recommended for the low–high dichotomy. It is even possible that variation in the choice of checklist might produce different quality assessments for the same studies. Getting worried?

With this background, it should be clear that the published guides on critical appraisal of studies for evidence-based practice, or on study quality assessment for systematic reviews, are mostly of a generic nature. Ultimately, it is our responsibility to adapt them to our review considering the issues specific to our questions. If we are lucky, existing reviews on the same topic may have already developed a suitable quality checklist. In this situation re-invention would be pointless and using an existing checklist would also enhance comparability with other reviews on our topic. On the other hand, if there are no suitable existing checklists, we will have to develop one. We will need to identify the individual items for assessing quality carefully and judiciously. How can we recognize which items are important for our review? Studies relevant to the review question may be susceptible to specific biases related to the way in which they are conducted and their data analysed. Therefore, we will have to be prepared to modify a relevant generic quality checklist, including appropriate additional items and deleting irrelevant ones. Following the approach shown in Box 3.1, the examples in Boxes 3.3 and 3.4, and the demonstrations in case studies 2 to 4, we should be able to develop a reasonable quality assessment checklist for our review.

3.1.1 Key biases in research addressed by generic quality assessment items

There are many generic biases that reviewers need to consider when developing quality assessment checklists. Bias has been defined as a tendency in research to produce results that depart systematically from the 'true' results. There are several types of biases. Here we shall consider four key biases which impact on the (internal) validity of a study. These are selection bias, performance bias, measurement bias and attrition bias (Box 3.2). Ideally, researchers should

> **Bias** either exaggerates or underestimates the 'true' effect of an *intervention* or *exposure*.

try to avoid these biases altogether in primary studies, but we know that they don't. Therefore a very good understanding of these issues must be developed in order to be able to discover biases during study quality assessment in our review. Our efforts may be made difficult or even impossible due to the poverty of reporting in some studies.

A simple *study design* for an effectiveness study is shown in Box 3.2. An important requirement for valid results in these studies is that the comparison groups should be similar at the beginning. This is because when there is imbalance of relevant prognostic features between groups, it becomes difficult for differences in *outcomes* to be confidently attributed to the *intervention*. Technically speaking, this is due to confounding. It is at the time of allocating participants to groups that selection bias

> The (internal) **validity** of a study refers to the degree which its results are likely to be free of **bias**.

Box 3.2   Key biases and their relationship to the design and the quality of a study

A study design to assess the effectiveness of interventions

Simple description

A study that allocates (with or without randomization) subjects from a relevant *population* to alternative *interventions* and follows them up to determine the effectiveness with which *interventions* improve the *outcome*.

Study flow chart with key biases

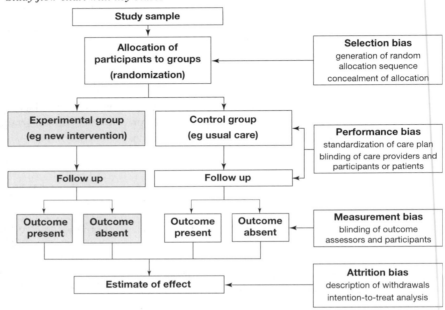

Key biases and their implications for quality assessment

Type of bias	Relevant generic quality items
Selection bias Systematic differences between comparison groups in prognosis or responsiveness to treatment.	• Generation of random sequence for allocating (large number of) participants to groups • Concealment of allocation from care providers and participants (this can also be done in unblinded studies)
Performance bias Systematic differences in care provided apart from the *intervention* being evaluated.	• Standardization of care protocol • Blinding of clinicians and participants

continued

Box 3.2   Key biases and their relationship to the design and the quality of a study (*continued*)

Type of bias	Relevant generic quality items
Measurement bias Systematic differences between comparison groups in how *outcomes* are ascertained.	• Blinding of participants and *outcome* assessors
Attrition bias Systematic differences between comparison groups in withdrawals from the study.	• Intention-to-treat analysis (or a complete description of withdrawals to allow such an analysis)

See Box 3.3 for generic quality items based on these biases

3

arises and it is important to check if appropriate measures were designed and implemented to prevent or minimize it. Experimental studies using random allocation of participants (with concealment of allocation sequence) produce comparison groups that are expected to be balanced for known, unknown and unmeasured prognostic variables. This is the main reason why there has been an emphasis in reviews to focus on randomized trials.

Following the allocation of participants to groups, performance bias may arise due to unintended *interventions* or co-interventions (eg other treatments which are not part of the research). We need to assess if the care plans were standardized and if the researchers and the participants were kept blind to the group allocation. We also need to examine if there was a risk of measurement bias, particularly if the *outcomes* assessed were subjective, and if the participants and researchers involved in ascertaining the *outcomes* were not blind to group allocation. In this way blinding is important for preventing both performance and measurement bias.

For preventing attrition bias, an intention-to-treat (ITT) analysis is needed, and it requires data for all patients. Participants' *outcomes* are analysed according to their initial group allocation, regardless of whether they fully complied with the intervention, changed their intervention group during the study or dropped out of the study before its completion. If the selected studies do not perform their analysis in this way, we may be able to do the calculation ourselves provided a complete description (numbers and reasons) of the withdrawals is available including information on both the people who dropped out and those lost to follow-up. If participants withdraw from the study and their *outcome* is unknown, there is

Confounding is a situation in comparative studies where the effect of an *intervention* on an *outcome* is distorted due to the association of the *outcome* with another factor, which can prevent or cause the *outcome* independent of the *intervention*.

In an **intention-to-treat (ITT) analysis**, subjects are analysed according to their initial group allocation, regardless of whether they fully complied with the intervention, changed their intervention group after initial allocation or left the study early.

Box 3.3 Example of developing a quality assessment checklist in an effectiveness review

1) **Define the clinical question and the selection criteria**
   Free form question: Among infertile couples with subfertility due to a male factor, does anti-estrogen treatment increase pregnancy rates? (*see structured question in Box 3.5*)

2) **Define the selection criteria**
   - Nature of question   Assessment of clinical effectiveness
   - *Study design*   Comparative studies (*see Box 1.4*)
   - *Study design* threshold   Inclusion criterion: experimental studies
                                    Exclusion criterion: observational studies

3) **Develop the quality checklist**
   a) Generic quality items for the checklist (see Box 3.2)
   Generation of a random sequence for allocating the patients to the *interventions*
   - Adequate
   - computer generated random numbers or random number tables
   - Inadequate
   - use of alternation, case record numbers, birth dates or week days
   - Unclear or unstated

   Concealment of allocation
   - Adequate
   - centralized real-time or pharmacy-controlled randomization in unblinded studies, or serially numbered identical containers in blinded studies
   - other approaches with robust methods to prevent foreknowledge of the allocation sequence to clinicians and patients
   - Inadequate
   - use of alternation, case record numbers, birth dates or week days, open random numbers lists, or serially numbered envelopes (even sealed opaque envelopes can be subject to manipulation)
   - Unclear or unstated

   Blinding
   - Adequate
   - care provider and study patients
   - Inadequate
   - care provider or study patients or neither
   - Unclear or unstated

   Description of withdrawals (to allow an intention-to-treat (ITT) analysis)
   - Adequate
   - inclusion of all those who dropped out/were lost to follow-up in the analysis
   - numbers and reasons provided for each group
   - description allows analysis following the ITT principle
   - Inadequate
   - only numbers (not reasons) provided for each group
   - description does not allow an analysis following the ITT principle
   - Unclear or unstated

   continued

Box 3.3   Example of developing a quality assessment checklist in an effectiveness review (*continued*)

b) Specific quality items related to the clinical features of the review question

The population	Complete diagnostic work-up for infertility
The interventions	No relevant items
The outcome	One year follow-up duration to detect pregnancy

4) **Incorporate the quality assessments into the review**

Some examples of the above quality assessment are as follows:

• To describe the quality of studies included in the review (*see Box 3.5*)

• To aid in determining the strength of inferences (*see Box 5.3*)

3

no satisfactory way to perform the analysis. The options available include carrying forward the last *outcome* assessment or imputing the best or worst *outcome* for the missing observations in a sensitivity analysis. Thus if too many participants are lost to follow-up the analysis may produce biased effects.

Box 3.3 shows how key generic biases can be considered along with biases arising from issues specific to a review concerning the effectiveness of a treatment for infertility. In this example, good quality research requires that couples have a complete set of investigations for infertility before the *interventions* are provided and that they are followed up for long enough to allow detection of pregnancy. In this way it would be possible to assess if the treatment led to pregnancies more often than the control without the biasing influences of poor diagnostic work-up for infertility and inadequate length of follow-up. These issues are considered along with the generic key biases to produce a checklist for study quality assessment (see Boxes 3.3 and 3.5).

As indicated earlier, the biases related to selection, performance, measurement and attrition are some of the key biases and they pertain mainly to questions about effectiveness. If our question is about accuracy of tests (case study 4) or cost effectiveness (Box 3.4) or some other aspect of health care, we will have to consider the biases relevant to these research types for our quality checklist.

Withdrawals are participants or patients who do not fully comply with the intervention, receive an alternative intervention, choose to drop out or are lost to follow up. **Intention-to-treat** analysis with an appropriate **sensitivity analysis** is required to deal with withdrawals.

3.2   Quality assessments in reviews with a mixture of *study designs*

In the past there has been a strong emphasis for reviews to focus on a single *study design* of the highest quality, ie randomized controlled trials (Box 1.4). However, reviewers soon realized that for many important questions, studies of

Sensitivity analysis involves repetition of an analysis under different assumptions to examine the impact of these assumptions on the results. In a primary study where there are **withdrawals**, a sensitivity analysis may involve repeating the analysis imputing the best or worst *outcome* for the missing observations or carrying forward the last *outcome* assessment.

Effectiveness is the extent to which an *intervention* (therapy, prevention, diagnosis, screening, education, social care, etc.) produces beneficial *outcomes* under ordinary day-to-day circumstances.

Efficiency (cost effectiveness) is the extent to which the balance between input (costs) and outputs (*outcomes*) of *interventions* represents value for money.

high quality *designs* were often not available (case study 2) or they were scarce (case study 3). This is either because no one undertook such studies in the past or if they did try, it was not practicable or ethical to conduct them. When there is a dearth of studies with a high quality *design*, it is not uncommon for reviews to include a mixture of *designs* to summarize the available evidence. This approach carries problems in evidence synthesis (Step 4) and interpretation (Step 5). However, reviews including studies with multiple *designs* need not be confusing, particularly if due attention can be given to the quality assessment issues.

When using the approach described in Box 3.1 we might find that in some reviews, where the question demands studies of various *designs* to be included, the quality assessment will not be so straightforward. A mixture of studies with different *designs* may become part of a review because more than one *design* is needed to address the same question or because more than one question is to be addressed. Case study 3 presents an example where studies of both experimental (randomized and non-randomized) and observational (cohort study with concurrent controls) *designs* are included in a review to address a question about effectiveness. Here it is possible to develop and use a single checklist for quality assessment (Boxes C3.3 and C3.4). Some reviewers prefer to use separate checklists for different *designs* and this is the most reasonable approach in some situations; for example, when a review addresses two separate but related questions, eg about clinical effectiveness and efficiency of an *intervention*. This is like having two reviews in one. Here different quality assessments will have to be developed for the different *study designs* relevant to the two questions, as shown in Box 3.4.

3.3   Reliability of the quality checklist in a review

The evaluation of quality items is very often affected by vague and ambiguous reporting in the selected studies. In order to avoid subjectivity and errors when extracting information about quality, the review protocol should provide a clear description of how to assess quality. This would mean designing data extraction forms with clear and consistent coding of responses. Ideally the forms should be piloted using several reviewers and a sample of studies to assess the reliability of the quality assessment process. Pilot testing might identify confusion about the extraction and coding instructions, which would then need to be clarified – a more explicit system of coding would improve inter-reviewer agreement.

In the past, people have suggested blinding the reviewers to the names of the authors, institutions, journals and year of publication when assessing quality. This should avoid bias as judgements about quality may be unduly influenced by these factors. Therefore some reviewers go to great lengths to have such identifying

Box 3.4 Example of developing a quality assessment checklist in a review with multiple questions.

1) **Define the question and the selection criteria**

Free form question: To what extent is the risk of postoperative infection reduced by antimicrobial prophylaxis, in patients undergoing hip replacement and is it worth the costs? (*see structured question in Box 1.3*)

- Nature of question

    Assessment of clinical effectiveness

    Assessment of cost effectiveness (or efficiency)

    – cost effectiveness can be assessed by (a) review of all available full economic evaluations, (b) a review of effectiveness studies in conjunction with any available cost sources, and (c) a secondary economic evaluation using the evidence from the effectiveness review to build an economic decision model. In this example we consider quality assessment for option (a).

- Study design

    Effectiveness: experimental studies

    Cost effectiveness: full economic evaluations

- Study design threshold

    Effectiveness: (*see Box 1.4*)

    – inclusion criterion: experimental studies

    – exclusion criterion: observational studies

    Cost effectiveness: (*see glossary*)

    – inclusion criterion: cost effectiveness analyses

    – exclusion criterion: partial economic evaluations

2) **Develop the quality checklist**

Some generic quality items for checklists

- Clinical effectiveness review
    - random allocation of patients to groups
    - concealment of allocation sequence
    - prespecified criteria for eligibility of patients
    - similarity of groups at baseline regarding prognostic factors
    - blinding of care providers, patients and *outcome* assessors
    - an intention-to-treat analysis

- Cost effectiveness review
    - a comprehensive description of alternative interventions
    - identification of all important and relevant costs and *outcomes* for the interventions
    - use of established evidence of clinical effectiveness, ie *intervention* known to improve *outcome*
    - costs and *outcomes* measured accurately and valued credibly
    - costs and *outcomes* adjusted for differential timing
    - an incremental analysis of costs and *outcomes*
    - sensitivity analyses for uncertainty in costs and *outcomes*

information masked before examining the manuscripts. However, the cumbersome and time-consuming procedures required to produce blinded papers have not been shown to impact on the conclusions of reviews and unmasked independent quality assessment by more than one reviewer should be sufficient. By now it should be quite clear that it is unwise to undertake a review without co-authors.

3.4 Using quality assessments in a review

Having developed our checklist and extracted the relevant data on quality assessment, we are ready to integrate this information in our review (Box 3.1). How would we describe the quality of the studies? There are many imaginative ways of presenting information about how the studies included in a review have complied with the quality items. Examples of quality description are shown in the case studies (Boxes C2.2, C3.4 and C4.4). We may start by describing how many studies meet the various quality criteria and support this with graphs, eg using stacked bar charts (Box 3.5). However, tabulation of the information on quality items for each one of the included studies is the clearest way to describe quality (Box 3.5).

One difficult issue in quality assessment is that of ranking studies according to their quality. A simple way is to rank studies according to the proportion of total items they comply with. When studies satisfy the same proportion of quality items, but are deficient in different areas, there is a problem. Here the deficient areas should guide us about the rank: studies with deficiencies in areas with a greater potential for bias (eg lack of concealment of allocation) should be ranked lower than those with deficiencies in areas with a smaller risk (eg deficiencies in allocation sequence generation). Weighting of items has been proposed but there are no agreed weighting schemes that apply universally. This is because the importance of quality items varies from topic to topic. For example, blinding is crucial in studies with subjective *outcomes*, but not so essential in those with objective *outcomes*.

Reviewers have to use their judgement when ranking studies according to quality in

---

Box 3.5 Example of tabulation and graphic presentation of study quality assessment

Free form question: Among infertile couples with subfertility due to a male factor, does anti-estrogen treatment increase pregnancy rates?

Structured question
- The population   Couples with subfertility due to a male factor (low sperm count)
- The interventions   Anti-estrogen treatment (clomiphene citrate or tamoxifen) for the male partner
                                       Comparator: placebo, no treatment, or vitamin C
- The outcomes   Pregnancy
- The study design   Experimental studies

continued

Box 3.5   Example of tabulation and graphic presentation of study quality assessment (*continued*)

Tabulation of study quality

Information about quality items can be placed in columns with the studies in rows (sorted according to year of publication).

Author	Year	Randomization		Blinding	Descripton of withdrawals	Population complete workup	Outcome 1-year long follow-up	Rank order of quality*
		Sequence generation	Concealment					
Roonberg	1980	Unstated	Unstated	Unclear	Adequate	Adequate	Inadequate	3
Abel	1982	Unclear	Unclear	Inadequate	Adequate	Unclear	Inadequate	4
Wang	1983	Unclear	Unclear	Inadequate	Unclear	Adequate	Adequate	6
Torok	1985	Unclear	Unclear	Unclear	Unclear	Inadequate	Adequate	5
Micic	1985	Unclear	Unclear	Inadequate	Unclear	Inadequate	Inadequate	9
AinMelk	1987	Unclear	Unclear	Unclear	Unclear	Inadequate	Inadequate	8
Sokol	1988	Adequate	Adquate	Adequate	Unclear	Adequate	Adequate	1
WHO	1992	Adequate	Adequate	Adequate	Adequate	Adequate	Inadequate	2
Karuse	1992	Unclear	Unclear	Inadequate	Unclear	Inadequate	Inadequate	7

* see text for an explanation

Bar chart of study quality

Information on quality presented as 100% stacked bars. Data in the stacks represents the number of studies meeting the quality criteria

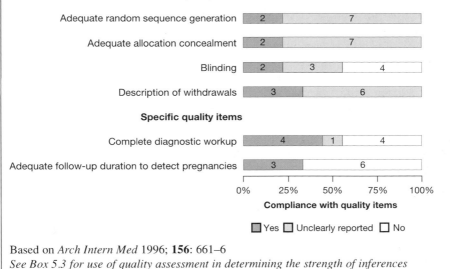

Based on *Arch Intern Med* 1996; **156**: 661–6
See Box 5.3 for use of quality assessment in determining the strength of inferences

the context of their topic. For example, in a review concerning effectiveness of a treatment for infertility (Box 3.5), two studies (Sokol and WHO) comply with five out of six quality items. Sokol is 'unclear' about its description of withdrawals and WHO has not followed participants up for one year (in fact they only followed up to 8 months). If we feel that adequacy of follow-up is more important than lack of clarity about the description of withdrawals, then we can rank Sokol higher than WHO. This subjectivity cannot be removed from reviewing, so it is important that judgements are made before the results of the studies are known. This example should also make it clear that there are limits to how detailed judgements can be. Often it is impossible to have a sensible ranking of studies according to quality and one may have to settle for a more crude categorization, eg high vs low quality studies, as in case study 2. Having performed quality assessments in a sensible (and unbiased) manner, one can confidently proceed to data synthesis (Step 4), interpretation of results and generation of inferences (Step 5) where variation in the quality of the selected studies may have important implications. We see examples of how strength of inferences is linked to quality assessment in Boxes 5.2 and 5.3.

Summary of Step 3: Assessing quality of the literature

Key points about appraising review articles

- Examine the methods section to see if a study quality assessment has been undertaken.
- Has quality been used as a criterion for study selection? (Step 2)
- Has a more detailed assessment of the selected studies been carried out? Are the quality items appropriate for the question? Check the results section and the tables to see how much variation in quality there is between studies.
- Is the variation in quality an explanation for heterogeneity? Is meta-analysis appropriate given the quality? (Step 4)
- Is the strength of inferences linked to quality? (Step 5)

Key points for conducting reviews

- Obsession with quality is the 'Achilles heel' of all research studies and reviews. Quality assessment plays a role in every step of a review.
- Question formulation (Step 1) and study selection criteria (Step 2) should have *study design* components in them to determine the minimum acceptable level of study quality.
- For a more refined quality assessment of selected studies, checklists should be developed which consider the generic issues relevant to the *study design* aspects of the review question. These items may be derived from existing critical appraisal guides and *design*-based quality checklists.
- It is important to consider issues relevant to the *populations*, *interventions* and *outcomes* specific to the question. Considering these specific issues, the existing generic items may be modified or deleted and new relevant items may be added to the quality checklists.
- These detailed quality assessments will be used for describing the selected studies, exploring an explanation for heterogeneity (Step 4), making informed decisions regarding suitability of meta-analysis (Step 4), assessing the strength of inferences (Step 5) and making recommendations for future research.

Step 4

Summarizing the evidence

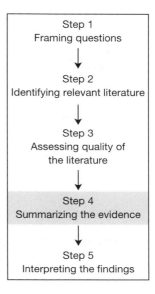

Step 1
Framing questions

↓

Step 2
Identifying relevant literature

↓

Step 3
Assessing quality of
the literature

↓

Step 4
Summarizing the evidence

↓

Step 5
Interpreting the findings

Collating the findings of studies included in a review requires more than just tabulation and meta-analysis of their results. It requires a deeper exploration and an in-depth analysis, for which the findings need to be presented in a clear way. We need to evaluate whether the observed effects of *interventions* are consistent among the included studies, and if not, why not? We need to assess if a statistical combination of individual effects (meta-analysis) is feasible and appropriate. These analyses allow us to generate meaningful conclusions from the reviews. This Step covers the basics of producing evidence summaries in systematic reviews, limiting the discussion to questions about the effects of *interventions* or *exposures* on binary *outcomes*. Once the principles are understood, they can be applied with appropriate tailoring to other question types (see case study 4).

4.1 Description of data contained in the included studies

To begin with, a descriptive summary of the findings of studies included in a review is required. In simple terms, the objective of this initial exercise is to present (in a meaningful way) the information about studies' characteristics (*populations*, *interventions* and *outcomes*), their *design* and quality, and their effects. There is no need to use any advanced statistics at this stage. We may use tables, figures and simple computations, such as proportions, relative risks, etc. which allow us to glance at the evidence and to glean the differences between studies. This is a crucial part of evidence synthesis; it will help us gain a deeper understanding of the evidence and should prevent errors in interpretation. It will also enhance the transparency of our analysis.

> **Effect** is a measure of association between an *intervention* or *exposure* and an *outcome*. The term **individual effects** means effects observed in individual studies included in a review. **Summary effect** means the effect generated by pooling individual effects in a meta-analysis.

When faced with large amounts of data to be summarized, tabulation can be a daunting task. The process of carrying out the tabulations should follow from the review question. The nature and complexity of the table depends a great deal on how many studies are included and how much data needs to be displayed from each. The decisions about the structure of the tables should be guided by what we considered to be important issues at the time of question formulation and what, in our judgement, could produce a variation in effects (as outlined in Step 1). So, for example, information may be tabulated with studies in rows grouped according to a characteristic of the *population*. Then information on *interventions*, *outcomes* and effects for each study could be summarized succinctly (Box 4.1).

Box 4.1 Tabulating information from studies included in a systematic review

Suggested steps

1. Place features related to *populations*, *interventions* and *outcomes* in columns.

2. Consider what subgroups of *populations* there are among included studies.

3. Consider what subtypes of *interventions* there are.

4. Consider the *outcomes* and if these could be used to produce subgroups.

5. Consider if studies need to be subclassified according to *study designs* and quality.

6. Populate the cells in the table with information from studies along rows in subgroups.

7. Sort studies according to a feature that helps to understand their results (eg a characteristic of a *population* or *intervention*, rank order of quality, year of publication, etc).

8. Also consider an open column for 'comments'.

An example of tabulation of studies in a review of antimicrobials for chronic wounds
This is only a brief tabulation. Detailed tables can be found in the report of the review available at www.hta.nhsweb.nhs.uk/htapubs.htm

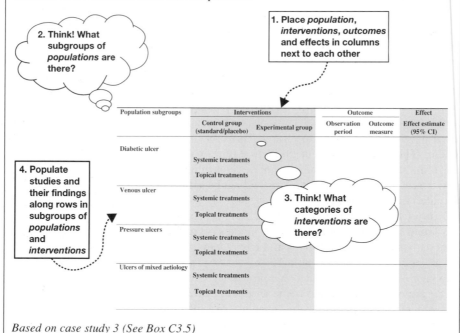

Based on case study 3 (See Box C3.5)

Sometimes tables will end up with too many columns to fit on one page. In this situation it is often helpful to breakdown the tabulation into several tables. We may produce one detailed table of *population* characteristics and relevant prognostic factors; another table may include details of *interventions* and yet another for details of *outcomes*. The features of *study designs* and other aspects of study quality may be presented in a separate table or a figure (Box 3.5). Preparation of tables is often laborious and time consuming, but without them we cannot understand the results of the included studies. Once the hard work is done, a quick scan through these tables should allow us, and more importantly others, to judge how studies differ in terms of *populations*, *interventions*, *outcomes* and quality.

At this stage, we should also compute and tabulate the effects found in each one of the studies along with their confidence intervals (Box 4.2). This will help us examine the direction and magnitude of effect among the individual studies. By direction of effect we mean either benefit or harm. By magnitude we mean how much benefit or how much harm. Box 4.3 shows how to evaluate direction and magnitude of effect graphically in a forest plot.

A simple tabulation of numerical results, like the one shown in case study 3 (Box C3.5), is not easy to assimilate at a glance. Therefore, it is worth examining the effects graphically (Box 4.3). These graphic summaries would help us make qualitative judgements about the effects of *interventions*, particularly about the direction, magnitude and precision of the individual effects. Occasionally, this may produce a surprise: a conclusion about effectiveness may be reached solely from qualitative examination of the observed effects without the need for statistical analysis, particularly if there are numerous studies with consistent and large effects. In this situation a quantitative synthesis (meta-analysis) may not add anything to our inferences. However, often the effects will not be precise enough because of a small sample size in individual studies. The graphic display will give us a good idea about effectiveness but this will not be sufficient to generate inferences. Here, meta-analysis will be useful, as it will improve the precision of the effect by statistically combining the results from individual studies – but first we need to assess if the effects vary from study to study (heterogeneity) and if it is sensible to undertake a meta-analysis.

One aim of data description is to assess the extent of the evidence in order to plan statistical analyses. We should have planned our analyses for heterogeneity and meta-analysis in advance, and armed with information from the tables we

The **direction of effect** indicates a beneficial or a harmful effect. The point estimate of an effect tells us about direction and magnitude of the effect.

The **precision of effect** relates to the degree of uncertainty in the estimation of effect that is due to the play of chance. The confidence interval tells us about precision.

Point estimate of effect is its observed value in a study.

Confidence interval is the imprecision in the point estimate, ie the range around it within which the 'true' value of the effect can be expected to lie with a given degree of certainty (eg 95%).

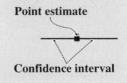

Point estimate

Confidence interval

Box 4.2 Estimation of effects observed in individual studies included in a systematic review

Measures of effect

An effect is a statistic, which provides a measure of the strength of relationship between an intervention and an outcome, eg relative risk (RR), odds ratio (OR), or risk difference (RD) for binary data; mean difference or standardized mean difference for continuous data; and hazard ratio for survival data (see glossary). Statistical significance tells us nothing about the magnitude of the effect. Effect measures help us to make judgements about the magnitude and clinical importance of the effects. The term 'individual effects' means the effects observed in individual studies included in a review. 'Summary effect' means the effect generated by pooling individual effects in a meta-analysis.

Computing effect measures for binary outcomes in individual studies

Computing point estimates of effects is relatively simple as shown below. With several studies to compute effects for and estimating confidence intervals for every effect, makes manual calculation tedious. We would suggest using a statistical software package. We have generally used RevMan, the Cochrane Collaboration's review management software, to compute and present results in this book (www.cochrane.org/cochrane/revman.htm).

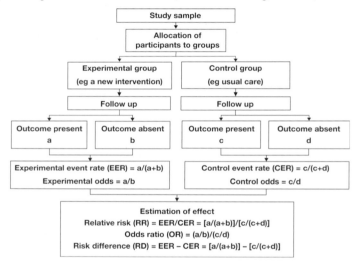

Choosing an effect for binary outcomes

The choice depends on the ease of interpretation and statistical properties of the effect measure. Clinicians prefer relative risk (RR) and number needed to treat (NNT) – which is the inverse of risk difference (RD) – because they are intuitive. Some statisticians prefer OR because it is not sensitive to the reversibility of the event classification and it is more suitable for statistical manipulation and modelling. RR and OR are relative measures of effect and, compared to RD, they tend to be more consistent in systematic reviews when studies have considerable variation in control event rate. The summary NNT (and summary RD) values generated from meta-analyses can be seriously misleading as their meaningful clinical application depends on the knowledge of baseline rates in the *population*s where the results are to be applied (see Step 5). We will often be faced with OR in the medical literature. From these we can generate NNTs for interpretation as shown in Box 5.5.

Box 4.3   Summarizing the effects observed in studies included in a systematic review

Forest plot
This is a commonly used, easy to understand, graphical display of individual effects observed in studies included in a systematic review (along with the summary effect if meta-analysis is used, as in Box 4.4). For each study, a box representing the point estimate of effect lies in the middle of a horizontal line which represents the confidence interval of the effect. When using relative risk (RR) or odds ratio (OR) as the effect measure, the effects are usually plotted on a log-scale. This produces symmetrical confidence intervals around the point estimates. A vertical line drawn at an RR or OR value of 1.0 represents 'no effect'. For desirable outcomes (eg pregnancy among infertile couples) RR or OR value >1.0 indicates that the experimental intervention is effective in improving that outcome compared to the control intervention. However, most reviews report undesirable outcomes (eg death) and then RR or OR values <1.0 indicate an advantage for the experimental group. A confidence interval overlapping the vertical line of 'no effect' represents lack of a statistically significant effect.

Description of effects and their uncertainty in a systematic review
Free form question: Among infertile couples with subfertility due to a male factor, does anti-estrogen treatment increase pregnancy rates? *(see structured question in Box 3.5)*

The effects observed among nine studies
Effects summarized as RR and OR, sorted by year of publication. Effect values >1.0 indicate an advantage for the treatment group compared to control, ie pregnancy rates improve with anti-estrogen treatment.

4

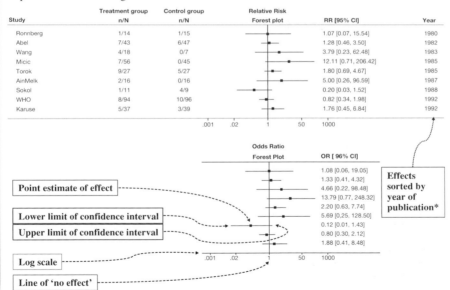

Based on *Arch Intern Med* 1996; **156**: 661–6.
Review manager software used to compute effects and produce graphics (www.cochrane.org/cochrane/revman.htm). It is developed by the Cochrane Collaboration and is available as a free download. Technical support is provided only for Cochrane reviewers.
*See Box 5.3 for a Forest plot with studies sorted according to rank order of quality.

Sensitivity analysis involves repetition of an analysis under different assumptions to examine the impact of these assumptions on the results. In a systematic review where important information about methods and data is missing from the included studies, it may involve a reanalysis of the review's findings taking into account the uncertainty in methods and data.

should be able to assess their feasibility. We will be able to see if data on clinically important *outcomes* are available for the *interventions* we wanted to compare. We may become aware of additional issues of importance, which were not known at the planning stage. If we decide to pursue these issues, we should be honest about reporting them as post-hoc analyses and we should be conscious of the problems of spurious significance associated with them. Our enquiry might be limited due to lack of data or due to missing information on important issues. It might be useful to contact the authors of individual studies before proceeding further; alternatively we could plan a sensitivity analysis to take account of the uncertainties due to missing or unclear information.

4.2 Investigating differences in effects between studies

There are usually some differences between studies in the key characteristics of their *populations*, *interventions* and *outcomes* (clinical heterogeneity), and their *study designs* and quality (methodological heterogeneity). These are discovered during tabulation of information from the studies. These variations in study characteristics and quality are likely to have some influence on the observed effects. Investigation for heterogeneity is about this variation of effects between studies and its reasons.

We may begin exploring for the possibility of heterogeneity of effects between studies by studying the tables we produced earlier. However, we will probably get a better idea about heterogeneity by visually examining the forest plot for variations in effects (Box 4.3). In general, if the point estimates of effects lie on one side of the 'line of no effect', then the *interventions* can be expected to produce the same qualitative effect, either benefit or harm. If the point estimates are located on both sides of the 'line of no effect', then they could produce beneficial and harmful effects (as in Box 4.3). Clearly this should raise suspicion about heterogeneity. We should also see if the confidence intervals of the effects overlap each other. If they do, as in Box 4.3, then it is more likely that any differences in the point estimates of effects are merely due to chance or indicate only limited heterogeneity, which is unavoidable.

Formal statistical tests for heterogeneity examine if the observed variability in effects is compatible with that expected to occur by chance alone. The chi-square test for heterogeneity among the effects shown in Box 4.3 has a *p*-

Question components

The *population*: A clinically suitable sample of patients

The *interventions*: Comparison of groups with and without the *intervention*

The *outcomes*: Changes in health status due to *interventions*

The *study design*: Ways of conducting research to assess the effect of *interventions*

value of 0.36 – well above the conventional threshold of $p<0.05$. These tests tend to have low power so they might miss important between-study differences in effects. It has therefore been suggested that a less stringent threshold of $p<0.1$ should be used to statistically assess heterogeneity. A reasonable approach would be to take non-statistical assessment of heterogeneity seriously – do not rely on p-values alone. Whenever we suspect substantial heterogeneity, we should seek an explanation, whether or not heterogeneity is statistically confirmed. We will turn to exploring reasons for heterogeneity shortly, but first we take a look at the basics of meta-analysis.

Heterogeneity is the variation of effects between studies. It may arise because of differences in key characteristics of their *populations*, *interventions* and *outcomes* (clinical heterogeneity), or their study *designs* and quality (methodological heterogeneity).

4.3 Meta-analysis (quantitative synthesis) of effects observed in studies

As indicated earlier, individual studies may be far too small to produce precise effects and so meta-analysis can improve precision by combining them statistically. First we must determine if meta-analysis is at all possible, and if so, whether it would be appropriate. By examining the tables produced for describing the studies we will be able to determine if the data necessary to perform a meta-analysis are available. Sometimes meta-analysis will just not be feasible, for example when there are important differences between the studies in terms of *populations*, *interventions*, *outcomes*, *designs* and quality, it would be senseless to try to estimate a summary effect (as in case study 3). A systematic review does not always have to have a meta-analysis! In addition, by examining for differences in effects between studies, we will be able to determine whether or not the studies are too heterogeneous to be sensibly combined. We should proceed with meta-analysis only if the studies are similar in clinical characteristics and methodological quality, and are homogeneous in effects.

In a meta-analysis, in simple terms, the effects observed across studies are pooled to produce a weighted average effect of all the studies – the summary effect. As a general principal, each study is weighted according to some measure of its importance, eg a method that gives more weight to more informative studies (often larger studies with precise effect estimates) and less weight to less informative studies (often smaller studies with imprecise effect estimates) is used. In most meta-analyses, this is achieved by assigning a weight to each study in inverse proportion to the variance of its effect. Averaging effects across studies in this

Power is the ability of a test to statistically demonstrate a difference when one exists. When a test has low power, a larger sample size is required, otherwise there is a risk that a possible difference might be missed.

Variance is a statistical measure of variation measured in terms of deviations of the individual observations from the mean value.

The **inverse of variance** of observed individual effects is often used to weight studies in statistical analyses used in systematic reviews, eg meta-analysis, metaregression and funnel plot analysis.

Meta-analysis is a statistical technique for combining the individual effects of a number of studies addressing the same question to produce a summary effect.

way ensures that the *intervention* groups within each study are only compared to the control groups in the same study. Thus, in a meta-analysis of experimental studies, the benefit accrued by randomization (with allocation concealment) is preserved when the results are pooled. An example meta-analysis is shown in Box 4.4.

It is important to be familiar with the finer points concerning pooling individual effects in a meta-analysis

---

Box 4.4 Summarizing the effects using meta-analysis

Forest plot of individual and summary effects
Effects observed in individual studies are plotted along with the summary effect. For each study, the point estimate of effect is a box of variable size according to the weight of the study in the meta-analysis. The summary effect is plotted below the individual effects using a different graphic pattern, eg a filled diamond (the width of the diamond represents the confidence interval and the centre of the diamond represents the point estimate).

An example meta-analysis using fixed and random effects models
The example shown below is based on the question and the effects (relative risk, RR) described in Box 4.3. Compared to the fixed effect models, the random effects models produce wider confidence interval around the summary effect because they take into account between-study variability. They also preferentially weight smaller studies, which have more varied effects than larger studies.

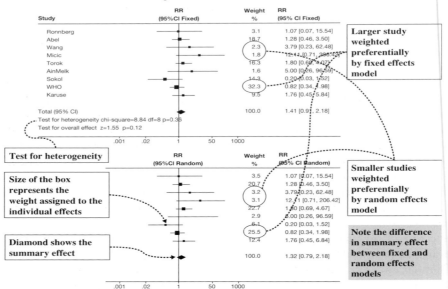

Based on *Arch Intern Med* 1996; **156(6)**: 661–6
Review manager software used to compute effects and produce graphics
See Box 5.3 for subgroup meta-analysis.

because we will be faced with them regularly when reading or conducting reviews. During a meta-analysis it is essential to check how robust our summary effect is to the variation in statistical methods. There are two concepts to keep in mind: the 'fixed effect' and 'random effects' statistical models.

A fixed effect model estimates the average effect assuming that there is a single 'true' underlying effect. A random effects model assumes that there is no single underlying value of the effect, but there is a distribution of effects depending on studies' characteristics. The differences between effects are considered to arise from between-study variation and the play of chance (random variability). A random effects model weights smaller studies proportionally higher than a fixed effect model when estimating a summary effect. This phenomenon may exaggerate the impact of publication bias and poor quality in smaller studies.

When computing confidence intervals, random effects models incorporate the variance of effects observed between the studies (assuming that they have a normal distribution). Hence, when there is heterogeneity, a random effects model produces wider confidence intervals of the summary effect compared with a fixed effect model. Therefore it can be argued that the fixed effect model may give undue precision to the summary effect (a spuriously narrow confidence interval) if there is significant unexplained heterogeneity between the studies. In the example meta-analysis shown in Box 4.4 summary effects generated with both fixed and random effects models are demonstrated. In practice both statistical models may be used to assess the robustness of the statistical synthesis, but if we have to make a choice we should do this *a priori* and not after we have been biased by knowledge of the results.

4.4 Clinical heterogeneity

Differences in the characteristics of the studies with respect to *populations*, *interventions* and *outcomes* can provide useful answers regarding heterogeneity and can help in interpreting the clinical relevance of the findings. The exploration of these differences can be facilitated by constructing the summary tables in such a way that potential explanations for differences in effects can be more easily identified. During question formulation (Step 1), we would have identified important issues that could produce a variation in effects (see examples in Box 1.3). Based on this information, we may stratify the studies into subgroups according to *populations*, *interventions* and *outcomes* sets. The differences in effects in the various subgroups of studies can then be explored.

If there are many studies in our review, the differences in effects may also be examined statistically, as shown in Box 4.5. We can perform a meta-analysis of subgroups of studies and additionally examine if the effects are consistent within the subgroups. Advanced statisticians could also determine the statistical significance (*p*-value) of the difference in the effect between subgroups, however, this is beyond the scope of this book. We should be aware that investigations into the reasons for heterogeneity must be interpreted with caution. As with statistical tests for detection of heterogeneity, tests for evaluating its reasons also have limited power so they may

Box 4.5 Exploring clinical heterogeneity

Subgroup analysis

Free form question: Do home visits improve the health of elderly people?

Structured question

- The populations — Elderly people in various age groups
- The interventions — Home visits of various intensities and frequencies
  Comparator: usual care
- The outcomes — Mortality, functional status and nursing home admissions
- The study design — Experimental studies

Delineation of various subgroups (*considering the detailed question structure in Box 1.3*)

Subgroups	Age based subgroups	Assessment intensity based subgroups	Follow-up frequency based subgroups
• The populations	Elderly people in various age groups	Elderly people	Elderly people
• The interventions	Home visits	Home visits of various assessment intensities	Home visits of various frequencies of follow-up
	Comparator: usual care	Comparator: usual care	Comparator: usual care
• The outcomes	Mortality	Functional status	Nursing home admissions

Subgroup meta-analyses

A vertical line in the centre of the diamond indicates the point estimate of the summary relative risk (RR) for each subgroup of studies with particular characteristics. The width of the diamond represents the confidence interval of the summary RR for each subgroup. RR values of <1.0 represent an advantage for the intervention group compared to control.

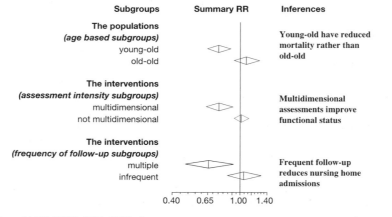

Based on *JAMA* 2002; **287**: 1022–8

miss a relationship. Another problem is that if too many subgroup analyses are carried out, some might be spuriously significant, a problem inherent in multiple analyses of any type. Therefore examination of the explanation for heterogeneity should be planned for a small number of study characteristics for which there is a strong suggestion of a relationship with the size of effect. In addition, the choice of subgroups should be made in advance (Step 1). It is good to be cautious – from examining the tables we generated earlier we might become aware of issues and possible relationships we had not anticipated. The temptation would be to undertake further subgroup analyses that were not originally planned. These post-hoc analyses should be avoided. If we cannot resist the temptation, they should be clearly identified and their findings should be interpreted cautiously. They should not be used to guide clinical practice but they can be used to generate hypotheses for testing in future research.

Where substantial heterogeneity is present and clinical reasons for it can be found, an overall meta-analysis is unnecessary. In this situation, meta-analysis should be restricted to clinically relevant subgroups where a variation in effect was originally anticipated. This approach will aid in clinical interpretation and application of the review's findings as highlighted by the example shown in Box 4.5.

4.5 Methodological heterogeneity

We should also find out if *design* and quality differences among studies appear to be associated with variation in their effects. This is important not only to explore reasons for heterogeneity, but also to assess the strength of our inferences. This is covered in detail in Step 5 and demonstrations of some exploratory methods are shown in Boxes 5.2 and 5.3.

If differences in study quality provide an explanation for heterogeneity, an overall meta-analysis should not be contemplated. If such a meta-analysis is undertaken, there is a risk that biased summary effects may be produced due to undue weighting of studies with inferior *designs* or quality. In an attempt to counter such a bias, the idea of weighting studies in proportion to their quality (rather than size or precision as described earlier) has been suggested. However, no agreed standards exist for producing such weights, so we should abandon this idea. Sometimes the only feasible approach will be a descriptive evidence summary, particularly if there are no subgroups of studies of a similar quality, but if there are, use a subgroup meta-analysis. Inferences should always be based on the effects observed in high-quality subgroups of studies (Step 5).

A technique for exploring heterogeneity called meta-regression is becoming fashionable, so we should touch on it briefly, mainly with a view to helping with critical appraisal. Put simply, this technique fits a multivariable linear regression model for examining the influence of study characteristics and quality on the size of individual effects observed among studies included in a review. In this way it searches for the unique contribution of different variables towards an explanation for heterogeneity. Meta-regression does have a down side – it suffers from the risk of what is described in regression analysis as 'overfitting'. This arises because reviews often only have a small number of studies and a large number of variables are available for inclusion in the model. In this situation, if a regression model is used, it will lead to spurious findings. So beware! The most powerful way to assess between-study differences is based on an analysis using individual patient data from the included studies. However, this is only rarely possible.

4.6 Meta-analysis when heterogeneity remains unexplained

Hopefully studies included in our review will not have any obvious heterogeneity. If we do encounter it, hopefully our exploration for reasons behind the heterogeneity will bear some fruit. However, in many reviews there will be no explanations, neither clinical nor methodological. In this situation one might say that heterogeneity remains unexplained despite a sensible exploration. This may be because the number of studies in a review is not large enough to allow a powerful analysis to decipher the reasons behind differences in effects between studies. Now, do we or do we not perform meta-analysis? There is no simple answer.

Publication bias is said to arise when the likelihood of the publication of studies and thus their accessibility to reviewers is related to the significance of their results regardless of their quality.

We should ask ourselves what is to be gained by meta-analysis. Can we not interpret the studies' findings with tabulation and forest plots of individual effects? The temptation would be to attribute the heterogeneity to chance variation between studies and then undertake meta-analysis using a random effects model as this approach accounts for the variation between studies that cannot be explained by other factors. If you do succumb to this temptation (which happens far too often), proceed with caution. Make sure to look for and exclude funnel asymmetry (Box 5.1), a factor indicative of publication and related biases (Step 5). Otherwise a random effects model may produce biased summary effect estimates. In addition, our interpretation of the summary effect should be cautious as heterogeneity limits the strength of inferences that can be drawn from reviews (Box 5.4). We must examine to see if the overall summary effect and the effects of the high quality subgroup of studies are, by and large, consistent. Even when meta-regression provides no apparent reason for heterogeneity, the results of high-quality studies may be different. In this way quality becomes a critical factor in the interpretation of findings of a review and the strongest inferences in a review are those that are based on high-quality studies (Step 5).

Summary of Step 4: Summarizing the evidence

Key points about appraising review articles

- Examine the methods and results sections to see if heterogeneity of effects is evaluated.
- Was the exploration for heterogeneity planned in advance?
- Is variation in clinical characteristics of the studies an explanation for heterogeneity?
- Is variation in *study design* and quality an explanation for heterogeneity?
- Is meta-analysis appropriate in the light of information gathered on heterogeneity and its reasons?

Key points about conducting reviews

- The aim of this step is to collate and summarize the findings of studies included in a review.
- Data synthesis consists of tabulation of study characteristics, quality and effects as well as use of statistical methods for exploring differences between studies and combining their effects (meta-analysis) appropriately.
- Tabulation of evidence helps in assessing feasibility of planned statistical syntheses and improves overall transparency.
- Exploration of heterogeneity and its sources should be planned in advance.
- Exploration of clinical heterogeneity should be based on a small number of study characteristics for which there is a strong theoretical basis for a relationship with the effect.
- Exploration of methodological heterogeneity should consider factors for which there is strong theoretical or empirical basis for suspecting a relationship with bias. (Step 5)
- The following questions should be considered prior to embarking on meta-analysis: Is meta-analysis feasible given clinical heterogeneity? Is meta-analysis feasible given the variation in study quality?
- If an overall quantitative summary is not feasible, subgroup meta-analysis might be feasible and could provide clinically useful answers.

4

Step 5

Interpreting the findings

Step 1
Framing questions
↓
Step 2
Identifying relevant literature
↓
Step 3
Assessing quality of
the literature
↓
Step 4
Summarizing the evidence
↓
Step 5
Interpreting the findings

Deciphering the salience of a review's findings is as much art as it is science. The ultimate purpose of a review is to inform decision-making, and the big question at the end of a systematic review is 'how can one go about making decisions with the collated evidence?' However, the task of generating meaningful and practical answers from reviews is not always easy. We will cover some of the key issues that aid sensible and judicious interpretation of the evidence, avoiding both over- as well as underinterpretation.

By the time our review is nearing completion or after having read someone else's review, we may think that we already know the meaning of the findings. But what are the main findings? The answer to this question may not be as straightforward as we might think in the first instance. There may be numerous findings relating to various subgroups of *populations*, *interventions* and *outcomes* within the review. The principal findings should be related to the main questions formulated in Step 1. Other findings should be considered secondary.

Next we will need to consider the validity of the main findings. This will depend on the strengths and weaknesses of our review. We will need to consider how well the review complies with the key points on appraising reviews at the end of each Step in this book, such as:

- Are the searches adequate?
- Is there a risk of publication and related biases?
- Is the quality of the included studies high enough?
- Are the observed effects of substantial clinical, not just statistical, significance?

Answers to these and other related questions will allow us to make judgements on how much trust we can have in the findings of the review and what they mean. Following this we should be able to generate inferences and recommendations for clinical practice as well as for future research.

In this step we will cover four key issues: examining the risk of publication and related biases, determining the strength of the review's main findings, grading recommendations and generating clinically meaningful evidence summaries that aid with application of the evidence in clinical practice.

The *population*: A clinically suitable sample of participants

The *interventions*: Comparison of groups with and without the *intervention*

The *outcomes*: Changes in health status due to *interventions*

The *effect*: A measure of association between *interventions* and *outcomes*

5.1 Exploring for publication and related biases

Publication bias is said to arise when the likelihood of publication of studies and thus their accessibility to reviewers is related to the significance of their results regardless of their quality.

How can we be sure that our review does not suffer from publication and related biases? Hopefully a systematic approach has been used to track down studies, whether they are published or not (Step 2). Hopefully, the search has particularly focussed on capturing those studies that are less accessible, eg through searching multiple databases, and has not used language restrictions in study identification. Hopefully, the net cast is wide enough to capture all relevant studies (or at least an unbiased sample of the relevant literature). However thorough the literature search is, there cannot be any guarantees. But there can be some comfort (or discomfort) from formal post-hoc assessment for publication and related biases in a review.

A simple, perhaps too simple, but commonly used method of exploring for these biases is based on the so-called 'funnel plot' analysis. To perform this analysis meaningfully numerous studies, including some large studies, are required. As shown in Box 5.1, it is a scatter plot of individual effects that are observed among studies

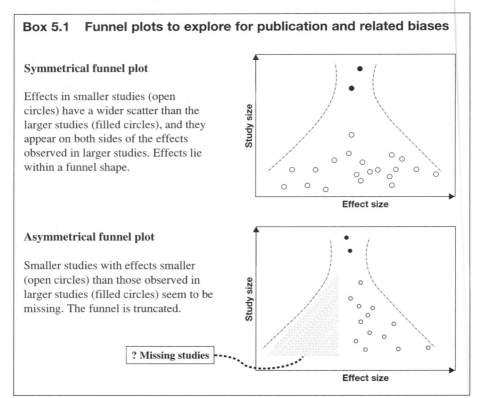

Box 5.1 Funnel plots to explore for publication and related biases

Symmetrical funnel plot

Effects in smaller studies (open circles) have a wider scatter than the larger studies (filled circles), and they appear on both sides of the effects observed in larger studies. Effects lie within a funnel shape.

Asymmetrical funnel plot

Smaller studies with effects smaller (open circles) than those observed in larger studies (filled circles) seem to be missing. The funnel is truncated.

? Missing studies

included in a review against some measure of study information (eg study size, inverse of variance). If all the relevant studies ever carried out are included in our review, the scatter of data points in the plot can be expected to lie within a funnel shape. The funnel is inverted when the y-axis is taken to represent study size (or inverse of variance) as in Box 5.1. This is because there is a wider range of effects among smaller studies compared to the effects observed among larger studies. In this situation the funnel is said to be symmetrical and we can have more confidence that publication and related biases are unlikely in our review. If the funnel is truncated, a group of studies may be missing from our review. Usually missing studies are small in size with different effects to those observed in the large studies included in our review. Such omissions are unlikely to be due to chance alone and they make the funnel asymmetrical. Publication bias is just one of a host of related reasons for funnel asymmetry, including location bias, English language bias, database bias, citation bias, multiple publication bias, poor methodological quality of small studies and clinical heterogeneity (eg small studies in high risk populations) to name a few. Whatever the reason, our confidence in the findings of the review will be limited if there is a truncation of the funnel.

Variance is a statistical measure of variation, measured in terms of deviation of the individual observations from the mean value.

A number of statistical tests are available to examine if funnel asymmetry is likely to be due to chance. These are outside the remit of this book, but some advice will be helpful for critical appraisal of reviews. The shapes of funnel plots vary according to the measures of effect and study size, and statistical tests for asymmetry often don't give consistent results. So, to avoid overinterpretation, funnel plot analyses should only be considered exploratory in nature. If it is any consolation, the true extent of publication and related biases may never be known.

The **inverse of variance** of observed individual effects is often used to weight studies in the statistical analyses used in systematic reviews, eg meta-analysis, meta-regression and funnel plot analysis.

5.2 Determining the strength of a review's findings

Hopefully, *study design* will have been used as one of the selection criteria (Step 2). This way poor quality evidence would have been removed and the review would have focussed on studies of a minimum acceptable quality from the outset. So why should there be a fuss about basing a review's inferences on the quality of its component studies? In many reviews, depending on the type and amount of available literature, it is inevitable that selection criteria specifying the *study design* will allow inclusion of studies of methodologically inferior *designs* (Step 2). Even when search and selection focus on robust *study designs*, there will be some variation in quality between studies. This happens because the devil about quality is in the detail: the 'gross' hierarchies of evidence used for study selection do not capture finer points about quality which are important for the validity of the results.

Hopefully, we would have performed detailed study quality assessments and discovered the variation in quality between studies (Step 3). During study synthesis we should gauge if quality has an association with the estimation of effects as part of the exploration for heterogeneity and its sources (Step 4). The reason for being concerned about study quality and a review's inferences is that if we find different individual effects among studies of different quality, we can no longer trust the overall summary effect. If high quality studies produce conservative estimates of effect, our inferences would also have to be conservative.

In this section we expand on the brief description related to methodological heterogeneity provided earlier in Step 4. We may have got some idea about the relationship between quality and effects by tabulating the relevant information on quality and effects together. In fact, where studies of different *designs* are included in a review, we should tabulate the studies subgrouped according to *design*. In this situation, if a meta-analysis is (mistakenly) undertaken using studies of different *designs*, there is a risk that biased summary effects may be produced due to undue weighting of studies that are inferior in *design*. A meta-analysis should only be contemplated within subgroups of studies of the same *design* and inferences should be based on the effects observed among studies of superior *design*. As shown in Box 5.2, we might find that studies of superior *designs* do not show an association between *exposure* and *outcome* when studies of inferior *designs* do. Even when a review focuses on studies of a single *design*, there may be variation in effects according to quality. Often the relationship between quality and effect would result in detectable heterogeneity, but this is by no means the rule. If the effects of studies were stacked in decreasing order of quality in a forest plot, the relationship would become apparent. For example, an increase in effect may be observed as the quality deteriorates, as shown in Box 5.3.

> The **quality** of a study depends on the degree to which its design, conduct and analysis minimizes **biases**.

> **Bias** either exaggerates or underestimates the 'true' effect of an *intervention* or *exposure*.

We should explore the relationship between study quality and effects even when heterogeneity is not statistically demonstrable, because effects among high-quality studies may be different to those among low-quality studies (Box 5.3). There is some controversy about how to do this. Some experts consider it preferable to perform a subgroup analysis, stratifying the studies according to their compliance with individual quality items; but this has the disadvantage of increasing the number of subgroups (see case study 4), which in turn carries the risk of spurious statistical significance as indicated in Step 4. Alternatively, quality scores (composed with the quality items) may be used to stratify studies, but the scoring systems are usually not well developed (Step 3). If there is a good correlation between studies with regard to compliance (and non-compliance) with a number of quality items, it may be sensible to stratify studies into high- and low-quality subgroups based on compliance with most of the quality items (Box 5.3). This approach would reduce the number of subgroup analyses and minimize the risk of spurious findings. Hopefully, the analytical approach outlined in this section will enable us to understand the limitations that quality of the evidence places on our review's inferences.

Box 5.2 Using study design to gauge strength of inferences

Free form question: Is exposure to benzodiazepines during pregnancy associated with malformations in the new-born baby? (*also see Box 1.2*)

Structured question
- The population   Pregnant women
- The exposures   Benzodiazepines in early pregnancy
                           Comparator: no exposure
- The outcomes   Major malformations in the new-born baby
- The study design   Observational studies with cohort and case-control designs
                           (*see Box 1.4*)

Summary of evidence
There was statistically significant heterogeneity in the overall analysis. Overall summary odds ratio (OR) suggested a trend towards an association between exposure to benzodiazepines and the risk of major malformations in the new-born baby. We use OR in this analysis because among studies with case-control *design* it is not possible to compute risk and relative risk.

Exploring the impact of study design on the effects observed in the review

<table>
<tr><td>

Subgroup analysis stratified according to study design

The association between exposure to benzodiazepines in pregnancy and major malformations is only supported by the subgroup of case-control studies (where there is heterogeneity). These studies are of an inferior design compared to cohort studies. Among the sub-group of studies with cohort design (where there is no heterogeneity) there is no association.

Note: OR values >1.0 indicate an association of malformations with exposure to benzodiazepines compared to no exposure.

</td><td>

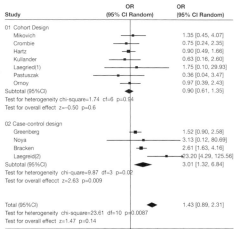

</td></tr>
</table>

Naïve inference without considering study design
Exposure to benzodiazepines in pregnancy is possibly associated with major malformations in the new-born baby.

Inference considering study design
Exposure to benzodiazepines in pregnancy is <u>not</u> associated with major malformations in the new-born baby.

Based on *BMJ* 1998; **317**: 839–43
RevMan software used to compute effects and produce graphics
See Box 4.4 for summarizing effects using meta-analysis

Box 5.3   Using study quality to gauge strength of inferences

Free form question: Among infertile couples with subfertility due to a male factor, does anti-estrogen treatment increase pregnancy rates? (*see structured question in Box 3.5*)

Summary of evidence (based on the review summaries in Box 4.3 and 4.4)
There was no statistically significant heterogeneity in the overall analysis. Summary relative risk (RR) suggested a trend towards an increase in pregnancy rate among couples treated with anti-estrogens.

Exploring the impact of study quality on the effects observed in the review

Forest plot with effects stacked in decreasing order of quality*

For high-quality studies there is a trend towards harm from treatment. As the quality of studies decreases this trend reverses and the possibility of benefit emerges.

Subgroup analysis stratified according to quality*

The beneficial trend in the overall meta-analysis is supported only by low-quality studies. High-quality studies suggest a trend towards harm, ie decrease in pregnancy rates, with treatment.

Note RR values >1.0 indicate an advantage for anti-estrogen treatment compared with control.

*See Box 3.5 for detailed quality assessment of individual studies and rank order.

Study	Relative Risk	RR [95% CI]
Sokol		0.20 [0.03, 1.52]
WHO		0.82 [0.34, 1.98]
Ronnberg		1.07 [0.07, 15.54]
Abel		1.28 [0.46, 3.50]
Torok		1.80 [0.69, 4.67]
Wang		3.79 [0.23, 62.48]
Karuse		1.76 [0.45, 6.84]
AinMelk		5.00 [0.26, 96.59]
Micic		12.11 [0.71, 206.42]

.001   .02   1   50   1000

Study	RR (95% CI Fixed)	RR (95% CI Fixed)
01 High quality studies		
Sokol		0.20 [0.03, 1.52]
WHO		0.82 [0.34, 1.98]
Subtotal (95% CI)		0.63 [0.29, 1.37]
Chi-square 5.03 (df=1) P: 0.02 Z=−1.16 P: <0.00001		
02 Low quality studies		
Ronnberg		1.07 [0.07, 15.54]
Abel		1.28 [0.46, 3.50]
Torok		1.80 [0.69, 4.67]
Wang		3.79 [0.23, 62.48]
Karuse		1.76 [0.45, 6.84]
AinMelk		5.00 [0.26, 96.59]
Micic		12.11 [0.71, 206.42]
Subtotal (95%CI)		2.10 [1.20, 3.66]
Chi-square 3.81 (df=6) P: 0.70 Z=2.61 P: 0.0001		
Total (95%CI)		1.41 [0.91, 2.18]
Chi-square 8.84 (df=8) P: 0.36 Z=11.55 P: <0.00001		

.001   .02   1   50   1000

Naïve inference without considering quality
Anti-estrogen therapy seems to have a trend towards a beneficial effect among infertile couples with subfertility due to a male factor.

Inference considering study quality
Anti-estrogen therapy has <u>no</u> beneficial effect among infertile couples with subfertility due to a male factor.

Based on *Arch Intern Med* 1996; **156**: 661–6
RevMan software used to compute effects and produce graphics
See Box 3.5 for a detailed description of quality
See Box 4.3 for a Forest plot with studies sorted according to year of publication
See Box 4.4 for summarizing effects using meta-analysis

5.3 Some pitfalls in grading recommendations for clinical practice

The usefulness of a review can be greatly enhanced by providing evidence-based 'bottom line' messages to healthcare practitioners. Generating graded practice recommendations from the findings of the studies summarized in a review may help achieve this objective and this approach is commonly used in clinical practice guidelines. There is considerable scope for confusion when converting evidence from reviews into graded recommendations. In this section we will give a brief overview of the potential problems to help with critical appraisal of reviews and guidelines.

Grading recommendations is important even when reviews are rigorously conducted. It is important to differentiate between recommendations that are based on strong versus weak evidence, which in turn depends on a number of factors including *study design* and quality. Evidence-based medicine has long emphasized the need to assess the strength of recommendations according to levels or hierarchies of evidence, which are based primarily on individual *study designs* (Box 1.4). Using this approach evidence may be classified as strong (Levels I and II), somewhat strong (Levels II and III) or not at all strong (Level IV). For the purpose of grading recommendations generated from the evidence, the levels can be converted from roman numerals into alphabetical (A, B and C) grades as shown in Box 5.4.

Evidence-based medicine (EBM) is the conscientious, explicit and judicious use of current best evidence in making decisions about health care.

The main attribute of this system is simplicity but 'things should only be made as simple as possible, without distorting their meaning, and no simpler'. It is too simple, perhaps even naïve, to classify recommendations into three letter grades based on *study design* only (Box 5.4). It does not consider precision of the effect when grading the recommendation. The greater the sample size, the more precise the effect, the narrower the confidence interval around the point estimate of effect, and the greater is the reviewers' ability to make a strong recommendation. And if the effects found are very large, moderate bias may not cancel such effects. Although the A, B and C grading system has been refined in various ways over the years, the simple system remains in extensive use. So beware! It can potentially be misleading.

The **precision of an effect** relates to the degree of certainty in the estimation of the effect.

The **confidence interval** tells us about precision as it gives the range within which the 'true' value of the effect can be expected to lie. Imprecision is related to random error arising from play of chance, not bias.

What we and other practitioners really want to know about recommendations in reviews is how credible they are. By credibility most people mean the authority to inspire, change or confirm belief. Readers of reviews want to be sure that the recommendations are not going to be suddenly reversed in the foreseeable future. The grading system should therefore take into account factors that make the recommendations durable. Of course *study design* is one factor that is pivotal in

LIVERPOOL
JOHN MOORES UNIVERSITY
AVRIL ROBARTS LRC
TITHEBARN STREET
LIVERPOOL L2 2ER
TEL. 0151 231 4022

Box 5.4 Grading recommendations for practice based on findings of reviews of effectiveness

Simple method of grading recommendations

This commonly used approach is based on *study design* and resultant levels of evidence (Box 1.4). It only pays lip service to refined and detailed quality assessments and it pays no attention to consistency of results from study to study and precision of the effects.

Grade	Study design*	Level of evidence*	Quality+	Heterogeneity§	Precision§
A	Experimental study	I, II	High	Consistent	Precise
B	Observational study	II, III	or	or	or
C	Expert opinion	IV	Low	Inconsistent	Imprecise

A proposal for an advanced method of grading recommendations

This approach uses all the available information in a systematic way. First it considers *study design* and related levels of evidence (Box 1.4) as above. Then it refines the grading according to the detailed quality assessments, consistency of results from study to study and precision of the effects.

Grade	Study design*	Evidence level*	Quality+	Heterogeneity§	Precision§
A+	Experimental study, randomized	I	High	Consistent	Precise
A−	Experimental study, randomized	I	High	Consistent	Imprecise
			High	Inconsistent	Precise
			Low	Consistent	Precise
A−−	Experimental study, randomized	I	Low	Consistent	Imprecise
			Low	Inconsistent	Precise
A−−−	Experimental study, randomized	I	Low	Inconsistent	Imprecise
B+	Experimental study, non-randomized	II	High	Consistent	Precise
	Controlled observational study	II	High	Consistent	Precise
B−			High	Consistent	Precise
	Experimental study	II	High/Low	Consistent	Imprecise
			High/Low	Inconsistent	Precise
	Controlled observational study	II	High/Low	Consistent	Imprecise
			High	Inconsistent	Precise
B−−	Experimental study, non-randomized	II	High/Low	Inconsistent	Imprecise
	Controlled observational study	II	High	Inconsistent	Imprecise
B−−−	Controlled observational study	II	Low	Inconsistent	Imprecise
	Uncontrolled observational study	III	–	–	–
C	Case reports Pathophysiological studies	IV	–	–	–

* See Box 1.4 for hierarchies of study design and levels of evidence
+ Based on refined and detailed quality assessments outlined in Step 3
§ Based on analyses outlined in Step 4

determining the credibility of the evidence and the resultant recommendation, but it is not the only factor and it is only a crude marker of validity (Step 3). Indeed reviews that do not consider *study design* as a selection criterion for ensuring a minimum level of study quality will have very limited power to inspire any belief. So the soundness of the *study design* provides the foundation when we begin to contemplate grading recommendations. It should be just that, a foundation, nothing more and nothing less. We can build on this foundation in the process of grading. Good reviewers have usually done a lot more than just assess *study design*. They have undertaken refined and detailed study quality assessments (Step 3). They have investigated heterogeneity and its reasons (Step 4). They have improved the precision of the individual effects by meta-analysis (Step 4) and examined the relationship between study quality and estimation of effects (Step 5). Why not use all this information in grading recommendations? This way the recommendations are likely to have much more credibility.

In Box 5.4 we see an approach that takes more than just *study design* into account when grading recommendations, but this approach is not so simple. It involves the use of objective criteria but also subjective interpretation:

- How high should the quality of the studies be for the results to be valid?
- How consistent should the effects be across studies to be homogeneous?
- How big should the effect size be to be of significance in clinical practice?
- How narrow should the width of the confidence interval be to be precise enough?

Sometimes the answers are obvious. In case study 3, the selection criteria have ensured that studies have at least Level I and II *study designs*. But grading any recommendations as A or B would be a very simple approach. This is because most of the studies actually constitute Level II not Level I evidence. Even when Level I evidence exists, it is of low quality on detailed assessment. The studies are too heterogeneous to be sensibly combined in a meta-analysis. The individual effects are imprecise. The grading from our proposed system would be 'B−' for a majority of the studies, which hardly qualifies as a small improvement over grade C. Needless to say this evidence has very limited, if any, power of changing or confirming belief. We are so concerned about the credibility of the evidence that, despite a robust systematic review, we do not provide any recommendations for practice in resolution of the scenario in case study 3. We only propose the use of common sense and suggest the need for future research.

Another common problem in grading recommendations is seen when using the same grading system for different types of clinical questions. The way we investigate patients for making a diagnosis is different to the way we make decisions about the provision of therapy. Hence different *study designs* are needed to address questions about diagnosis and therapy. However, reviewers and practitioners do not always realize this difference and use the same criteria for grading therapeutic, diagnostic and other types of evidence. For example, answers to questions regarding prognosis, cost effectiveness and so on, are not all sought from randomized controlled trials. A different system for grading recommendations is required for these issues.

5

'One system fits all' is just another one of the oversimplifications when defining grades of recommendations.

5.4 Applying the findings of a review in a clinical setting

By this time we must be thinking that we have reached the end. We have undertaken a thorough literature search and examined for publication and related biases (Box 5.1). We have explored if studies with certain *population* and *intervention* features (such as the severity of the disease, the setting, the treatment intensity or timing) are associated with an improved or reduced size of relative effect (Box 4.5). We have considered the quality of studies included in the review and its impact on the strength of our inferences (Boxes 5.2 and 5.3). In this way, we already know if we can have sufficient trust in the review and we also have a good idea of the magnitude and range of the expected benefits (or harms or other *outcomes*) among certain *population* groups. If we are in a situation where the evidence in the review cannot be trusted (as in case study 3 where there are concerns about the quality of studies and the precision of effects) we cannot generate strong guidance for practice. However, if our evidence can be trusted, we need to do a bit more work before practical guidance can be generated.

How can we put a review's findings in clinically meaningful terms? We have measured the effects in relative terms (eg relative risk, RR; odds ratio, OR) as suggested in Box 4.2. Although the relative effect measures are useful for assessing the strength of the effect (and to perform meta-analysis), to judge whether an *intervention* is worthwhile, the absolute magnitude of the benefits, tailored to specific *population* groups, is needed. This permits for the clinical significance and the possible impact of the *intervention* to be understood. The absolute effect might be expressed as the risk difference (RD), which is a fraction, not a whole number. The average human brain can only interpret natural frequencies or whole numbers well. The reciprocal of RD converts a fraction into a whole number called the number needed to treat (NNT). However, this simple approach is only useful in dealing with data from individual studies. When using relative summary effect estimates obtained from reviews, the computation of the NNT is a bit more complicated. This is explained in Box 5.5, but first we examine some virtues of NNTs.

Decision-making in health care is influenced by many factors. The size of the effect and its statistical significance in a meta-analysis provide only part of the information required. For example, when we interpret the summary effect, having received information about our patient's risk of an *outcome* without treatment, we might decide not to use it in low-risk patients as in our judgement the treatment-associated morbidity and costs may not be worth the benefits. Thus, we may only use the treatment for patients at high risk. Relative effect measures tend to be constant across varying baseline risk so they are not as informative when tailoring treatment decisions. The NNT, however, is sensitive to changing baseline risks and it allows us to individualize the benefit of *interventions*. The higher the NNT, the greater the number of patients clinicians must treat to achieve a beneficial effect in one. Therefore they would be less inclined to recommend treatment and their patients would be more

Box 5.5 Individualizing summary effects from reviews to clinical scenarios

Free form question: Does aspirin in early pregnancy prevent later onset of hypertensive disorders?

Structured question
- The population   Women in early pregnancy
- The interventions   Low dose aspirin
                               Comparator: placebo or no treatment
- The outcomes   Hypertensive disorders of pregnancy
- The study design   Experimental studies (*see Box 1.4*)

Summary of evidence of effectiveness of aspirin (Based on *BMJ* 2001; **322**: 329–33) There were 32 relevant studies. Aspirin prevented hypertensive disorders of pregnancy with a summary relative risk (RR) of 0.85 (95% confidence interval 0.78–0.92). (RR values <1.0 indicate an advantage for aspirin treatment compared to control.)

Exploring variation in relative effects of aspirin among various risk groups

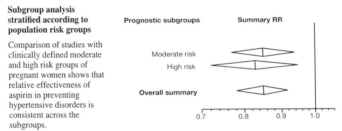

Individualizing aspirin prevention among various risk groups in early pregnancy Numbers of women needed to be treated (NNT) with aspirin to prevent hypertension in pregnancy may be computed for various risk groups defined according to the clinical history and the results of the Doppler ultrasound test. This would aid in decision making as one would be quite inclined to treat Doppler-positive women and not so inclined to treat Doppler-negative women according to the following NNTs.

Risk group	Baseline risk*	NNT⁺
Clinical history: high risk		
Doppler-positive	23.5%	29
Doppler-negative	7.8%	86
Clinical history: moderate risk		
Doppler-positive	18.8%	36
Doppler-negative	2.5%	267

*Based on a review of diagnostic accuracy of Doppler test in predicting pregnancy hypertension, *BJOG* 2000; **107**: 196–208
⁺ Computed using the following formula:
NNT = 1/[BR × (1-RR)], where BR is baseline risk and RR is 0.85
If the summary effect measure is odds ratio (OR), then the following formula is required:
NNT = [(1 −BR) + (OR × BR)]/[BR × (1-OR) × (1-BR)]

5

Baseline risk is the risk of *outcome* in a *population* without *intervention*. It is related to severity of the underlying disease and prognostic factors. Baseline risk is important for determining who will benefit most from the *intervention*.

Prognosis is a probable course or *outcome* of a disease. Prognostic factors are patient or disease characteristics that influence the course. Good prognosis is associated with a low rate of undesirable *outcomes*; poor prognosis is associated with a high rate of undesirable *outcomes*.

inclined to avoid treatment. Very often, in patients at higher baseline risk (ie worse prognosis), the NNT will be lower than in patients at lower risk (ie good prognosis). The lower the NNT, the smaller the number of patients clinicians must treat to achieve a beneficial result in one person; the more inclined a clinician would be to recommend treatment and the more enthusiastic their patients would be to have treatment.

How are NNTs generated from relative summary effects provided by reviews? A precondition is that the relative effects are in fact consistent across studies with varying baseline risks. Empirical evidence suggests that summary RR from meta-analysis using a random effects model is reasonably constant across various baseline risks. The same is true for summary ORs. If we want to explore this phenomenon in our review, a simple investigation requires a subgroup meta-analysis of studies stratified according to the prognostic category of the recruited patients. When such an analysis shows consistency in relative effects, we may use them to generate NNTs, as shown in Box 5.5. We will of course need information on our patient's clinical condition and prognosis, which may require us to draw on evidence outside our effectiveness review. We might find that the evidence of the review moderated by the patient's specific circumstances might lead to different applications in different patients. For example, considering the variation in NNTs among risk groups (outlined in Box 5.5), we might decide to treat Doppler-positive women but not Doppler-negative women within a clinically moderate-risk group. In the case studies and examples provided in this book, the interpretations of the evidence have been based on specific scenarios. Judicious interpretation of findings in other contexts may lead to different resolutions of scenarios.

Summary of Step 5: Interpreting the findings

Key points about appraising review articles

- What is the credibility or trustworthiness of the evidence?
- If the evidence in the review can be trusted, what is its meaning for clinical practice?
- Do the recommendations reflect strengths and weaknesses of the evidence?
- The article may not provide much of the analysis required for interpretation, but following the advice given in this Step, we might be able to generate clinically meaningful inferences for ourselves.

Key points about conducting reviews

- Ascertain that the key points about appraising reviews listed at the end of each of the four steps so far have been met.
- If feasible, funnel plot analysis should be undertaken to explore for the risk of publication and related biases.
- Exploration for methodological heterogeneity should help determine if the overall summary can be trusted and if not then the effects observed in high-quality studies should be used for generating inferences.
- Any recommendations should be graded considering all the strengths and weaknesses of the evidence, not just *study design*.
- Explore variations in the relative effects and their reasons, particularly if the relative effects vary with risk level or severity of disease. The intervention may be effective only in certain clinical groups.
- Compute the predicted absolute effects (numbers needed to treat, NNTs) according to disease severity. This way we will be able to individualize the effects observed in the review to the characteristics of our patients.

5

Section B
Case studies

The application of review theory covered in the preceding section is illustrated through the following case studies. Some readers may prefer to assimilate the review theory first before turning to the case studies. Others may read them in conjunction with the information contained in the previous section. Each case consists of a scenario requiring evidence from reviews, a demonstration of some review methods and a proposed resolution of the scenario. Insight into critical appraisal and conduct of a systematic review can be gained by working through the case studies.

- Case study 1: Identifying and appraising systematic reviews

- Case study 2: Reviewing evidence on safety of a public health intervention

- Case study 3: Reviewing evidence on effectiveness of therapy

- Case study 4: Reviewing evidence on test accuracy

Case study 1

Identifying and appraising systematic reviews

When seeking evidence from reviews to guide our clinical practice, we may face some difficulty in formulating questions. This is often due to the tension between addressing questions with either a wide or a narrow focus. Practitioners think broadly about clinical topics before making a decision for a specific patient or problem but evidence is not always summarized in this way. Nowadays we are likely to find several reviews on a question and awareness about variation in their focus is important.

This case study will demonstrate advantages and disadvantages of broad and narrow types of questions, and how to identify and appraise existing reviews. It will help us develop an approach to selecting relevant reviews when several reviews are available on a topic. It will draw on the key points about appraisal (shown at the end of each Step) to make our reading of reviews more efficient.

What is involved in identification, appraisal and application of evidence summarized in reviews?

Framing questions
↓
Identifying relevant reviews
↓
Assessing quality of the review and its evidence
↓
Summarizing the evidence
↓
Interpreting the findings

Scenario: Drug treatment for recent onset schizophrenia

You are a psychiatrist due to see a 25-year-old amateur guitar player who has a recent diagnosis of schizophrenia. This is a mental condition where the patient may suffer symptoms such as hallucinations (often hearing voices) and delusions (unshakeable beliefs that are contrary to a person's social and cultural background) called 'positive' symptoms. There may also be emotional numbness, lack of motivation, muddled speech and thoughts, which are called 'negative' symptoms.

Being a specialist, you are well aware of the various treatment options. These include the classical drugs such as chlorpromazine and haloperidol and a whole range of new antipsychotic drugs. The beneficial and harmful effects of these drugs are varied. New drugs are also more expensive. Given these variations, you had been thinking about examining the literature to check whether your prescribing practice was in line with the current best evidence. This case provides you with an opportunity to bring yourself up-to-date. To find out what the current state of affairs is concerning effectiveness and safety of antipsychotics you decide to examine some literature reviews. Having done your homework, you will be in a good position to consider the available options for this patient, taking account of her preferences. Playing music is the joy of

Effectiveness is the extent to which an *intervention* produces beneficial *outcomes* under ordinary day-to-day circumstances.

Question components
The *population*: A clinically suitable sample of patients.

The *interventions*: Comparison of groups with and without the *intervention*.

The *outcomes*: Changes in health status due to *interventions*.

The *study design*: Ways of conducting research to assess the effects of *interventions*.

her life; thus you are aware of the importance of avoiding treatments associated with movement disorders so that your patient's guitar playing is not impaired.

Step 1: Framing the question

Free form question

For adults with recent onset schizophrenia, what is the effectiveness of the various drug treatments and what are their harmful effects?

Structured question

The *populations*	Adults with recent onset schizophrenia (in this case study you are not interested in patients with unresponsive schizophrenia).
The *interventions*	Antipsychotic drugs both classical and new.
The *outcomes*	Beneficial: improvements on 'positive' and 'negative' symptoms. This may involve psychological measurements of global or mental state of the patient. Harmful: movement disorders and other side effects, eg somnolence.
The *study design*	Beneficial *outcomes*: review(s) of experimental studies addressing effectiveness. Harmful *outcomes*: review(s) of experimental and observational studies addressing safety.

The question formulated above is a broad one. Of the various components of the question, the *population* is quite focused, the *interventions* and *outcomes* are broad and so are the *study designs*. Both classical and new *interventions* (of which there are more than a dozen drug treatments), both beneficial and harmful *outcomes*, and both experimental and observational *designs* (Box 1.4) are to be considered. You expect to find a number of reviews, which have taken a narrower focus, eg comparing one drug versus another without regard for other available options. However, this would not be suitable for your case scenario. You want to choose a treatment for your patient with the optimum balance between beneficial and harmful effects after considering all available options.

Effect is a measure of association between an *intervention* and an *outcome*.

Step 2: Identifying relevant reviews

The number of reviews has increased exponentially in recent years. When searching for reviews to guide your practice, sometimes you may be faced with numerous reviews collating the findings of several studies on your topic of interest. Although this might fill you with enthusiasm, at the same time multiplicity of reviews presents a challenge. Identifying which reviews to read and which not to, may not be easy.

> A **Cochrane review** is a systematic review undertaken following the methodology of the Cochrane Collaboration and is included in the Cochrane Database of Systematic reviews in the Cochrane Library.

The Cochrane Library search

Having framed your question you decide to search the Cochrane Library. It has several databases, some of which have been shown in Box 0.1. It is the best source of reviews and protocols of reviews about effectiveness of interventions, which are included in its Cochrane Database of Systematic Reviews (CDSR). It also provides abstracts of quality assessed systematic reviews from a wide range of sources in the Database of Abstracts of Reviews of Effects (DARE), and abstracts of technology assessments from a network of agencies in the Health Technology Assessment (HTA) Database. In the fourth issue of the 2002 Cochrane Library there are:

- 1519 complete reviews
- 1136 protocols of reviews
- 2940 abstracts of quality assessed reviews
- 2838 abstracts of technology assessments.

There are several ways to find reviews in the Cochrane Library. Just by typing the words 'schizophrenia AND antipsychotics' in the query box of the Cochrane Library (2002, issue 3) and clicking the search button, you are pleasantly surprised to find 59 hits (50 reviews and 9 protocols) in CDSR and 14 hits in DARE (Box C1.1). In addition, there are three hits in the HTA Database. Scrolling down through CDSR you find several reviews, but they appear to address very focussed questions, much narrower than the question you have just formulated. However, among the 14 DARE abstracts, the first three titles appear to address a broad question similar to the one you are trying to answer. One of the HTA Database titles also seems relevant and it is the same as one of the three identified in DARE (Drug treatments for schizophrenia). For busy clinicians the most useful property of the DARE database is that assessment of the review's quality has already been carried out by trained staff who write the structured abstracts for this database. This may help you to decide which reviews to read in detail and, more importantly, which not to. So you take a look at what the abstracts in the DARE database have to say (Box C1.1).

Selecting a review to read in detail

From the titles of the DARE abstracts, it is clear that only three reviews have a broad focus compatible with your question. The key findings of the DARE abstracts concerning quality of their literature searches are provided in Box C1.1. The review in the *BMJ* searched comprehensively (though it reported unclearly about use of language restrictions) but it is not up-to-date. The other review in the *Annals of*

1

79

LIVERPOOL JOHN MOORES UNIVERSITY
LEARNING SERVICES

CASE

Box C1.1   Searching the Cochrane Library for systematic reviews on drug treatment for schizophrenia and selecting a review to read in detail

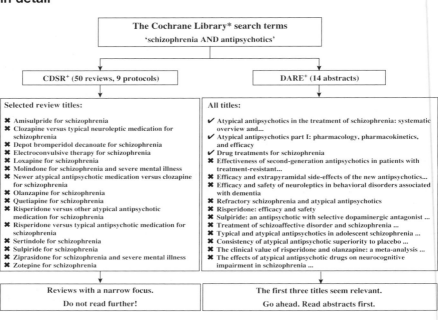

Selecting a review to read in detail

Review behind DARE abstract	Quality of its search	Decision to read further
Atypical antipsychotics in the treatment of schizophrenia: systematic overview and meta-regression analysis. *BMJ* 2000; **321**:1371–6.	MEDLINE, EMBASE, PsycLIT and the Cochrane Controlled Trials Register searched to December 1998. No description of language restrictions.	No, do not read further. Outdated.
Atypical antipsychotics part I: pharmacology, pharmacokinetics, and efficacy. *Annals of Pharmacotherapy* 1999; **33**: 73–85.	MEDLINE only searched from July 1986 to June 1998. Study selection restricted to English Language only.	No, do not read further. Outdated
Drug treatments for schizophrenia. *Effective Health Care Bulletin* 1999: **5**. (www.york.ac.uk/inst/crd/ ehc56.pdf)	Review of Cochrane reviews in the Cochrane Library 1999.	Yes. The bulletin available on the Internet indicates that an update has been commissioned. Obtain the most up-to-date review from www.hta.nhsweb.nhs.uk/

* Search results from the Cochrane Library 2002, issue 3
+ CDSR, the Cochrane Database of Systematic Reviews; DARE, the Database of Abstracts of Reviews of Effects. (See Box 0.1 for details)

Pharmacotherapy searched only one database; it used language restrictions in study selection and it is not up-to-date either. You decide to disregard both reviews.

The remaining review turns out to be a 'review of Cochrane reviews' which is not up-to-date either (last updated in 1999). Its abstracts in the DARE and HTA Databases provide a web link to its full report (www.york.ac.uk/inst/crd/ehc56.pdf). The report actually warns readers that its contents are likely to be valid for around one year following publication, by which time significant new research evidence may have become available. It also says that the review will be updated as part of the work for a forthcoming report commissioned by the UK National Health Service HTA Programme.

This information leads you the check the web pages of the HTA programme at www.hta.nhsweb.nhs.uk/. It appears that the above project has been superseded by a similar one commissioned by the HTA programme and data has recently been published (but it is not yet included in the Cochrane Library's HTA database). This review turns out to include no less than eight systematic reviews addressing benefits, adverse effects and cost effectiveness of new antipsychotics including amisulpride, clozapine, olanzapine, quetiapine, risperidone, sertindole, ziprasidone and zotepine. Given the fact that clozapine is a relatively old drug that was reintroduced for treating those with unresponsive schizophrenia, we leave it out of the rest of this case study. The reviews were actually based on updates of the Cochrane reviews that you already had identified in CDSR. You decide this must be the one for you and you will have a go at appraising this review yourself. This search also emphasizes the importance of checking if reviews have already been done or are in progress before even considering preparing a new systematic review.

Step 3: Assessing study quality

Given the large size of this report, and the fact that the included reviews have been prepared using the same protocols, you decide to take a two-step approach for your appraisal. First you check the quality of the overall report, and if satisfactory, you will then take a closer look at the amount and quality of the evidence included in each one of the reviews when interpreting the findings.

In this report the Cochrane reviews from 1999 had been updated with relevant studies found in comprehensive literature searches of more than 20 databases, 10 conference proceedings, ongoing trials registers, scanning of the reference lists of retrieved papers and reports of studies submitted by the companies which produced the drugs. In addition, further searches had been carried out for non-randomized studies of rare or long-term harmful outcomes. The quality of the included evidence was assessed by using separate checklists for effectiveness and safety studies. The studies were synthesized and interpreted in an appropriate way. Although assessment for the risk of publication and related biases had been limited because of scarcity of suitable data, the searches had been comprehensive enough to reassure you that this report provides the best available information. Based on the assessment of the methods used to

Safety relates to adverse events associated with *interventions*.

Box C1.2 Appraising the overall quality of a Health Technology Assessment report on systematic reviews of drug treatment for schizophrenia

Step 1: Framing questions
- The report is based on predefined questions.
- The questions were modified during the review, but justifications were provided.
- The questions do not seem to have been unduly influenced by knowledge of the results of studies.

Step 2: Identifying relevant literature
- The searches appear to be comprehensive. Over 20 databases, 10 conference proceedings, ongoing trials registers and the reference lists of retrieved papers have been searched. In addition, the companies that produce the drugs have submitted reports of their own studies.
- The selection criteria were set *a priori* and applied by two reviewers independently.
- It seems unlikely that relevant studies might have been missed.

Step 3: Assessing quality of the literature
- Quality assessment has been undertaken for studies included in the review.
- Quality has been used as a criterion for study selection (Step 2): for effectiveness, experimental studies were included and for safety, clear inclusion criteria concerning the *study designs* were formulated.
- A more detailed quality assessment of the selected studies has been carried out. The quality items seem to be appropriate for the question.
- Variation in quality has been explored as an explanation for heterogeneity and meta-analysis seems to have been used selectively where appropriate (Step 4).

Step 4: Summarizing the evidence
- Heterogeneity of effects has been evaluated.
- The exploration for heterogeneity was planned in advance in broad terms and with variations within the included systematic reviews.
- Variation in studies' clinical characteristics has been found to be an explanation for heterogeneity.
- Variation in *study design* and quality has also been found to be an explanation for heterogeneity.
- Meta-analysis seems to have been used selectively and appropriately in the light of information gathered on heterogeneity and its reasons.

Step 5: Interpreting the findings
- Risk of publication and related biases has been addressed in a limited way because suitable data were not available for all *outcomes*.
- There is no formal categorization of strength of inferences according to the quality of evidence, but the conclusions are clearly made with consideration of the quality of most studies.
- The credibility or trustworthiness of the evidence included in the review – the quality of included studies is limited and so is the number of relevant comparisons.
- The meaning of the review's findings for clinical practice – the review provides information that has limitations which make it difficult to generate durable inferences for practice.

Critical appraisal based on key points listed at the end of each Step in Section A of this book
The full review report is available from www.hta.nhsweb.nhs.uk/

undertake reviews in this report (Box C1.2), you are satisfied that they have been conducted to a high standard. You therefore feel that current decisions for practice can be based on the findings of the evidence included in the reviews.

Step 4: Summarizing the evidence

There were 171 experimental studies and 52 observational studies (addressing rare or long-term effects) in the review. However, the quality of the studies was not always ideal and the number of head-to-head comparisons evaluating similar *outcomes* was limited. An overview of the findings of the various reviews is provided in Box C1.3. The new drugs most frequently assessed for their effectiveness and safety were olanzapine and risperidone.

Beneficial effects

Evidence suggested that both classical and new antipsychotics had comparable levels of effectiveness. There were no clear differences in effectiveness between the various new antipsychotics. No single new antipsychotic agent stood out as being more effective than any of the others, nor did they collectively seem to be superior to classical drugs.

Harmful effects

The new antipsychotics possibly had fewer adverse effects in terms of movement disorders than the classical drug haloperidol. For example, risperidone showed a summary relative risk (RR) of 0.64 (95% CI 0.56–0.73) for 'movement disorders' based on seven studies. The new agents all seemed to have slightly different other side-effects which may vary in importance to those with schizophrenia and their carers.

Daytime sleepiness (somnolence) and drowsiness possibly occurred more frequently in those given clozapine or quetiapine than in those given classical drugs. Olanzapine, amisulpride, sertindole and perhaps risperidone may cause less somnolence than classical drugs. There was no evidence to suggest that the other new drugs were any more or less sedating than the classical drugs.

Step 5: Interpreting the findings

Even among rigorously conducted reviews, it is important to differentiate between strong versus weak evidence when interpreting the findings. Thus after reassuring yourself that this report is rigorous (Box C1.2), as a next step you decide to assess how robust its component reviews of individual drugs are. You use the key points from Step 5 and look at:

- quality of the studies within each review
- consistency of the observed effects in relation to variation in study quality
- precision of the effects, both beneficial and harmful.

1

CASE

Box C1.3 Assessing the quality of evidence included in systematic reviews of drug treatment for schizophrenia in a Health Technology Assessment report

	Total number of experimental studies		Effectiveness (alleviation of schizophrenic symptoms)		Safety (movement disorders and somnolence/drowsiness)	
	versus classical drugs	*versus* other new drugs	*versus* classical drugs	*versus* other new drugs	*versus* classical drugs	*versus* other new drugs
Amisulpride	13	4	Marginally better on most outcomes	No important differences	Less movement disorders	Few data, no clear differences
Olanzapine	24	14	Mostly marginally better	No important differences	Less movement disorders, less drowsiness	No clear differences
Quetiapine	9	1	Better on most outcomes, often marginally	Only one comparison available	Less movement disorders, may cause sleepiness	Very few data available
Risperidone	27	19	Better on most outcomes, often marginally	No important differences	Less movement disorders, less somnolence	Similar
Sertindole	2	0	No clear differences, few data	No comparisons available	Less movement disorders	
Ziprasidone	9	4	Few data in public domain*	Studies not in public domain*	Less movement disorders than haloperidol	Data not publicly available*
Zotepine	8	3	Equal or better results	Very few comparisons available	Less movement disorders, no differences for somnolence	Very few data available

The full review report is available from www.hta.nhsweb.nhs.uk/

*One governing body (UK National Institute for Clinical Excellence www.nice.org.uk/cat.asp?c=32878), after considering this evidence, concluded that for patients with newly diagnosed schizophrenia prescribing one of the following newer oral antipsychotic drugs should be considered: amisulpride, olanzapine, quetiapine, risperidone or zotepine. In drawing its conclusion, the governing body had access to confidential information which is not available in the public domain. Its recommendation is said to have a time limit of three years, after which it is likely to be reviewed again taking into account the newly accumulated evidence.

The available evidence for the effectiveness and safety of the new antipsychotics compared to classical drugs is, in general, of low quality and it is often based on short-term studies. The basis for choosing between the classical and the newer drugs is not as strong as one would like. However, for olanzapine and risperidone there is the biggest body of evidence and it suggests effectiveness comparable or better than classical drugs and similar to other new drugs. The evidence shows significant reduction in side-effects such as movement disorders and somnolence. Although the quality of the evidence is variable, when subgroup analysis is carried out on the highest quality studies available, inferences remain unchanged. Having considered the evidence yourself, you are more confident to use olanzapine or risperidone unless there were clear contraindications.

Resolution of scenario

Given the musical interest of your patient, you feel that a therapeutic choice based on avoiding movement disorders and somnolence makes sense as it would not interfere with her guitar playing. You decide to commence either olanzapine or risperidone with careful monitoring of the beneficial and harmful effects. If the treatment is not effective in alleviating symptoms or if there are unacceptable side-effects, you will switch to the other drug.

1

CASE

Case study 2

Reviewing evidence on safety of a public health intervention

Reviews of safety of interventions are not as common as those of their effectiveness. Research on safety may relate to common harmful outcomes, which may be captured in the same studies that address effectiveness. However, most experimental studies focus primarily on effectiveness and secondarily on safety – any information on safety is often only a by-product. Harmful outcomes can be rare and they may develop over a long time. There are considerable difficulties in designing and conducting safety studies to capture these outcomes, as a large number of people need to be observed over a long period of time. In this situation, observational not experimental studies are needed. With this background, systematic reviews on safety have to include evidence from studies with a range of *designs*.

This case study demonstrates how to seek and assess evidence on safety using a published review of a preventive public health intervention. This topic is important because public health interventions have an impact on large groups of populations and it has to be assured that the benefit outweighs any potential harm. This case study provides a demonstration of the application of review theory related to question formulation, literature identification and quality assessment of studies on safety.

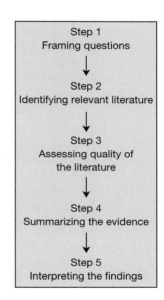

Step 1
Framing questions

↓

Step 2
Identifying relevant literature

↓

Step 3
Assessing quality of the literature

↓

Step 4
Summarizing the evidence

↓

Step 5
Interpreting the findings

Effectiveness is the extent to which an *intervention* produces beneficial *outcomes* under ordinary day-to-day circumstances.

Scenario: Safety of public water fluoridation

You are a public health professional in a locality that has public water fluoridation. For many years, you and your colleagues have held the belief that it improves dental health. Recently your local authority has been under pressure from various interest groups to consider the safety of this public health intervention because they fear that it is causing cancer.

Safety relates to adverse events associated with *interventions*.

In the past, most public health decisions have been based on judgement and practical feasibility, however, in recent years there has been an increasing demand to examine the scientific basis behind the issues under consideration. You have been observing this development with interest and now you have the chance to apply this

2

approach yourself. In anticipation of the discussion about the safety of water fluoridation intensifying in the near future, you want to prepare well and use evidence from the literature to inform any future decisions.

Using MEDLINE through the freely accessible PubMed interface (www.ncbi.nlm.nih.gov/entrez/query.fcgi), you enter 'drinking water fluoridation' into the query box and find 588 citations that may potentially provide information on your issue. Although you are a bit shocked about this large number of studies and are wondering how to squeeze the necessary reading time into your already packed daily routine, you perform a PubMed Clinical Queries search (www.ncbi.nlm.nih.gov/ entrez/query/static/clinical.html) using the same query in the Systematic Reviews feature. You find four citations; three are reviews and one is suitable for addressing your current concern:

- Systematic review of water fluoridation. *BMJ* 2000; **321**: 855–9. (seems relevant)
- Association of Down's syndrome and water fluoride level: a systematic review of the evidence. *BMC Public Health* 2001; **1(1)**: 6. (does not seem directly relevant)
- Exposure to high fluoride concentrations in drinking water is associated with decreased birth rates. *J Toxicol Environ Health* 1994; **42(1)**: 109–21. (does not seem directly relevant)
- Factors influencing the effectiveness of sealants – a meta-analysis. *Community Dent Oral Epidemiol* 1993; **21(5)**: 261–8. (does not seem relevant)

Incidentally if you undertook an Internet search the same day using the Google search engine (www.google.com), you will have an overwhelming 15 100 hits, but in the second position among them will be the full report of the systematic review on which the above *BMJ* paper is based:

Free form question: It describes the query for which you seek an answer through a review in simple language (however vague).

Structured question: Reviewers convert free form questions into a clear and explicit format using a structured approach (see Box 1.2). This makes the query potentially answerable through existing relevant studies.

- A systematic review of water fluoridation. NHS Centre for Reviews and Dissemination (CRD) Report 18. York, University of York, 2000 (available at www.york.ac.uk/ inst/crd/fluorid.htm)

Your impression is that using the review is the right starting point as it may save an enormous amount of time compared with obtaining and reading the large number of individual studies.

Step 1: Framing the question

Free form question:

Is it safe to provide population wide drinking water fluoridation to prevent caries?

Structured questions:

The *populations*   *Populations* receiving drinking water sourced through a public water supply.

The *exposures*   Fluoridation of drinking water (naturally or artificially) compared with non-fluoridated water.

The *outcomes*   Cancer is the main *outcome* of interest for the debate in your health authority. You also decide to consider other factors such as fluorosis (mottled teeth) and fractures as there has been concern about the effect of fluorides on bones.

The *study designs*   Comparative studies of any *design* (Box 1.4) examining the harmful *outcomes* in at least two *population* groups, one with fluoridated drinking water and the other without.

Question components

The *population*: A suitable sample of participants.

The *exposures*: Comparison of groups with and without the *exposure*.

The *outcomes*: Changes in health status due to *exposure*.

The *study design*: Ways of conducting research to assess the effect of *exposure*.

The original review was conducted to address five different questions. This case study will only focus (not least for the sake of brevity and simplicity) on the question of safety related to the *outcomes* described above.

Step 2: Identifying relevant literature

To cast as wide a net as possible to capture as many relevant citations as possible, a wide range of medical and environmental/scientific databases were searched to identify primary studies of the effects of water fluoridation (Box C2.1). The range of databases searched in this review is far beyond what is usually covered in reviews of clinical questions. The electronic searches are also supplemented by hand searching Index Medicus and Excerpta Medica for several years (back to 1945) to cover the time period before MEDLINE and EMBASE became accessible electronically. The search process was further supported by use of the Internet. Various Internet search engines were used to find web pages that might provide references. In addition, web pages were set up to inform the public about the review and to enable individuals and organizations to submit references or reports. Not surprisingly, there was a degree of duplication in the captured citations resulting from searching a wide range of databases. After the removal of duplicates, 3246 citations remained, from which the relevant studies were selected for review.

This comprehensive search of a variety of databases yielded far more citations than are commonly found when

Identifying relevant literature:
- Develop search term combinations
- Search relevant electronic databases
- Search other relevant resources
- Obtain full papers of potentially relevant citations
- Include/exclude studies using pre-set selection criteria

2

CASE

Box C2.1 Identification of relevant literature on safety of public water fluoridation

Electronic databases searched

1. Agricola
2. BIOSIS Previews (a database on life sciences)
3. CAB Health
4. CINAHL (Cumulative Index of Nursing and Allied Health Literature)
5. Conference Papers Index
6. EI Compendex (Engineering Index)
7. EMBASE (Excerpta Medica Database)
8. Enviroline
9. Food Science and Technology Abstracts (FSTA)
10. Health Service Technology, Administration and Research (Healthstar)
11. HSR Proj
12. JICST-E Plus (Japanese Science and Technology)
13. Latin American and Caribbean Health Sciences Literature (LILACS)
14. MEDLINE and OldMEDLINE
15. NTIS
16. PASCAL
17. PSYCLIT
18. Public Affairs Information Service (PAIS)
19. Science Citation Index and Social Science Citation Index
20. System for Information on Grey Literature in Europe (SIGLE)
21. TOXLINE
22. Water Resources Abstracts
23. Waternet

Study identification flowchart

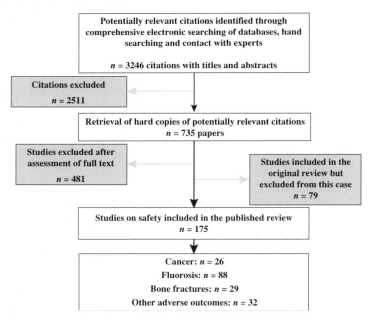

The original search is part of the full report of the review available at www.york.ac.uk/inst/crd/fluorid.htm

searching the literature for focussed clinical questions (compare with case study 3). The potential relevance of the identified citations was assessed – 2511 citations were found to be irrelevant. The full papers of the remaining 735 citations were assessed to select those primary studies in humans that directly related to fluoride in drinking water supplies, comparing at least two groups. These criteria excluded 481 studies and left 254 studies in the review. They came from 30 countries and were published in 14 languages between 1939 and 2000. Of these studies, 175 were relevant to the question of safety (Box C2.1).

Step 3: Assessing study quality

Study design threshold for study selection

Use of *study design* as a marker for ensuring a minimum level of quality has been described as an inclusion criterion in Step 2. This approach is easier to apply when seeking evidence of effectiveness using experimental studies. However, randomized studies are often difficult (if not impossible) to conduct at a community level for a public health intervention such as water fluoridation. Thus, systematic reviews assessing safety of such interventions have to look beyond experimental studies, and include evidence from various types of *study design*. Considering the nature of the research likely to be available to address safety issues, in this review a simple *design* threshold was used as a selection criterion: comparative studies of any design were included, but those without any comparative information were excluded (Box 2.4). In this way studies that provided information about the harmful effects of *exposure* to fluoridated water compared with non-*exposure* were selected.

Quality assessment of safety studies

After selecting studies of an acceptable *design*, their in-depth assessment for the risk of various biases allows us to gauge the quality of the evidence in a more refined way. The objective of the included studies is to compare groups *exposed* to fluoridated drinking water with groups without such *exposure*, and look for rates of undesirable *outcomes* without bias. Step 3 shows how to develop and use study quality assessments in a review of effectiveness. For safety studies to have validity, they must ascertain *exposures* and *outcomes* in such a way that the risk of misclassification is minimized. They must also establish the association between *exposures* and *outcomes*, adjusting for the confounding effect of other factors. These features are likely to be more robustly implemented in experimental studies, but they typically assess a relatively small number of participants over a short duration of follow-up. So in such studies there is only a limited chance of detecting rare *outcomes* that often do not

A **comparative study** is one where the effect of an *exposure* is assessed using comparison groups.

The **validity** of a study depends on the degree to which its *design*, conduct and analysis minimizes **biases**.

Bias either exaggerates or underestimates the 'true' effect of an *exposure*.

2

CASE

Confounding is a situation in comparative studies where the effect of an *exposure* on an *outcome* is distorted due to the association of the *outcome* with another factor, which can prevent or cause the *outcome* independent of the *exposure*. Data analysis may be adjusted for confounding in observational studies.

follow immediately after *exposure*. Hence quality assessment has to be planned somewhat differently than in reviews of effectiveness of *interventions*. In this case study the quality issues related to safety studies are briefly examined.

Anticipating that experimental studies would be scarce, reviewers planned study quality assessment based on features that would minimize biases of the various types described above. They assessed ascertainment of *exposures* and *outcomes*, ie how did the investigators make sure that the study participants had the *exposures* and *outcomes* under question. A prospective design would facilitate this. This means that those *exposed* (and *unexposed*) to fluoridated water and those developing cancer (and remaining free of cancer) are more likely to be correctly identified in these groups if they are assessed in a prospective fashion. The *exposure* is likely to be more accurately ascertained if the study commenced soon after water fluoridation and the *outcomes* are likely to be more accurately ascertained if the follow-up is long and if it is assessed blind to *exposure* status.

When examining how the effect of *exposure* on *outcome* was established, reviewers assessed if the comparison groups were similar in all respects other than their *exposure* to fluoridated water. This is because the other differences may be related to the *outcomes* of interest independent of the drinking water fluoridation, and this would bias the comparison. For example, if the people *exposed* to fluoridated water had other risk factors that make them more prone to cancer, the apparent association between *exposure* and *outcome* may be explained by the more frequent occurrence of these factors among the *exposed* groups compared with *non-exposed* groups. Technically speaking, such studies suffer from confounding. In a (large) experimental study, confounding factors are expected to be approximately equally distributed between groups (but no such studies exist on water fluoridation). In observational studies their distribution may be unequal. Primary researchers can statistically adjust for these differences when estimating the effect of *exposure* on *outcomes* (using multivariable modelling). If most important variables are adjusted for, it will be more likely that the observed association between *exposure* and *outcome* will be 'true'.

Put simply, use of a prospective design, robust ascertainment of *exposure* and *outcomes*, and control for confounding are the generic issues one would look for in quality assessment of studies on safety. Assessing these methodological features in safety studies of water fluoridation will require development of quality criteria specific to this topic. For example, studies commencing within one year of water fluoridation would be able to ascertain *exposure* better than those commencing within one to three years, which in turn will be better than those commencing after three years. This way studies would

Effect is a measure of association between an *exposure* and an *outcome*.

range from satisfactorily meeting quality criteria, to having some deficiencies, to not meeting the criteria at all, and they can be assigned to one of three prespecified quality categories as shown in Box C2.2.

Box C2.2 A quality assessment checklist for studies on safety of public water fluoridation

Quality assessment checklist

Quality issues	Quality categories	
	High* – Moderate	Low
Prospective design	Prospective	Prospective or retrospective
Exposure ascertainment	Study commenced within three years of water fluoridation	Study commenced after three years of water fluoridation
Outcome ascertainment	Long follow-up and blind assessment	Short follow-up and unblinded assessment
Control for confounding	Adjustment for at least one confounding factor	No adjustment for confounding factors

* High-quality studies were prospective, commencing within one year of water fluoridation, followed up people for at least five years, used blinding (or other robust methods) to ascertain outcomes and adjusted for at least three confounding factors (or used randomization) – no such studies existed.

Description of study quality
Information on quality presented as 100% stacked bars separately for studies evaluating different harmful outcomes. Data in the stacks represent the number of studies in moderate- and low-quality categories. There were no high-quality studies.

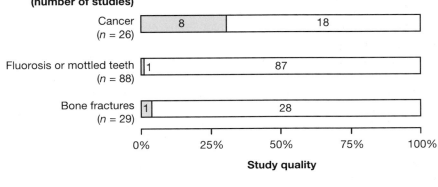

Description of quality of the selected studies

Based on the degree to which studies comply with the quality criteria, a quality hierarchy can be developed (Box C2.2). None of the included studies are in the highest quality category, but this is because experimental studies are non-existent and control for confounding is not always ideal in observational studies (none adjusted for three or more confounding factors in the analysis). Many studies lacked a prospective design, which makes ascertainment of *exposure* and assessment of *outcomes* difficult. More details of the study quality may be obtained from the review, but the general dearth of quality evidence in reviews of safety of interventions is not surprising to those experienced in this field.

The quality assessment for studies addressing the three harmful *outcomes* assigns low quality to the vast majority of the available evidence, only a few studies are classified as having medium quality, none have high quality (Box C2.2). Fortunately (because cancer is of major interest in this case study) studies examining the association between fluoridation and cancer show the highest quality as compared to those examining the other two harmful *outcomes* related to bones.

Step 4: Summarizing the evidence

Summarizing the evidence from studies with a large variety of designs and quality is not easy as highlighted in Steps 4 and 5. The review provides details of how the differences between study results were investigated and how they were summarized (with or without meta-analysis). This case study restricts itself to summarizing the findings narratively for harmful *outcomes*.

Cancer

The association between *exposure* to fluoridated water and cancer in general was examined in 26 studies. Of these, 10 examined all-cause cancer incidence or mortality, in 22 analyses. Eleven analyses found a negative association (fewer cancers due to *exposure*), nine found a positive association and two found no association. Only two studies found statistical significance. Thus, no clear association between water fluoridation and increased incidence or mortality was apparent. While a broad number of cancer types were represented in the included studies, bone/joint and thyroid cancers were of particular concern due to fluoride uptake by these organs. Six studies of osteosarcoma and water fluoridation found no statistically significant differences. Thyroid cancer was considered by only two studies and they also did not find a statistically significant association with water fluoride levels. Overall from the research evidence presented no association was detected between water fluoridation and mortality from any cancer or from bone or thyroid cancers specifically. These findings were also borne out in the moderate quality subgroup of studies.

Fluorosis

Dental flourosis is the most frequently studied harmful outcome, as reflected by the largest number (88) of studies included. Meta-regression analysis showed a strong (statistically significant) association between fluoride level and the prevalence of dental fluorosis.

Bone fractures

Twenty nine of the included studies investigated a variety of fracture sites; hip fracture was included in 18 of them. There are no definite patterns of association for any of the fractures. Similarly to the cancer studies, the studies showed similar numbers of positive and negative associations. Hip fracture analysed as a subgroup also showed no association with exposure to fluoridated drinking water.

Step 5: Interpreting the findings

In this case scenario, you focussed on safety of a community-based public health intervention. The generally low quality of available studies means that interpretation must be with appropriate caution. However, the elaborate efforts in searching an unusually large number of databases provide some safeguard against missing relevant studies and ongoing research. Thus we can have the confidence that the evidence summarized in this review is likely to be as good as it is going to get in the foreseeable future.

Cancer is the harmful *outcome* of most interest in the case scenario. No association is found between *exposure* to fluoridated water and specific cancers or all cancers. The interpretation of the results in this review may be limited because of the low quality of studies, but the findings for the cancer *outcomes* are also supported by the moderate-quality studies.

Fluorosis (mottled teeth) shows a simple association and also a dose–response relationship with increasing exposure to water fluoridation. When compared with a fluoride level of 0.4 ppm (parts per million), a level of 1.0 ppm had an estimated number needed to treat (NNT) of 6 (range 4–21), sometimes called number needed to harm (NNH) in this context. This means that on average, for every six people exposed to the higher concentrations of fluorides, one additional person had mottled teeth. Bone fractures do not show an association with water fluoridation.

Resolution of scenario

After having spent some time reading and understanding the review, you are impressed by the sheer amount of literature relevant to the question of safety. However, you are somewhat disappointed about the poor quality of the available primary studies. Of course, examining safety only makes sense in a context where the intervention has some beneficial effect. Benefit and harm have to be compared to provide the basis for decision making. Regarding the issue of the beneficial effect of public water fluoridation, you are reassured by the review that your prior belief and that of your health authority is correct: drinking water fluoridation does prevent caries. You can now go on to evaluate the findings of the review on safety – reduction in

2

CASE

caries by introducing fluoridation can be considered in context with cancer, fluorosis, bone fractures and other problems.

When the pressure from the interest groups raises the profile of the safety issue again, you will be able to reassure them that there is no evidence to link cancer with drinking water fluoridation. You will also be able to reassure them that research has not demonstated an increased risk of fractures to bones. However, you will have to admit the risk of dental fluorosis, which appears to be dose dependent. Those concerned about this issue can be given advice about examining their fluoride intake from other means. You may also want to measure the fluoride concentration in your area's water supply to openly share this information with the interest groups.

Being able to quantify the safety concerns of your population through a review, albeit from studies of moderate–low quality, allows your health authority, politicians and the public to consider the balance between beneficial and harmful effects of water fluoridation. For some, the prevention of caries is of primary importance, so they would prefer fluoridation. On the other hand, aesthetic reasons may play a more important role for others who would prefer to use other means of fluoride administration or even have caries removed occasionally rather than have mottled teeth. In any case, you are able to reassure all parties that there is currently no evidence of a risk of cancer or bone fractures from drinking water fluoridation.

Case study 3
Reviewing evidence on effectiveness of therapy

Not all reviews can provide answers that have immediate practical implications. And this may be due to a dearth of relevant studies. But lack of evidence of effectiveness should not be interpreted as evidence of lack of effectiveness.

This case study will demonstrate how to seek and assess evidence of therapeutic effectiveness in a review and how to act when faced with limited evidence. Based on a published review, it will provide a good demonstration of the application of review theory related to literature identification, quality assessment and study synthesis without meta-analysis.

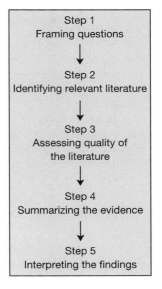

Scenario: Antimicrobial therapy for chronic wounds

You are a clinical research fellow in an academic primary healthcare practice. There are a large number of patients with chronic wounds of various aetiologies. You have taken it upon yourself to develop an evidence-based clinical strategy for use of antimicrobials in management of these patients. Your initial discussions with other members of the practice reveal that they base their management on:

- what they had learnt many years ago during medical school
- what they observed from the nurses on the wards during postgraduate training
- what they have been told by pharmaceutical company representatives.

Hardly anybody could underpin his or her advice by good evidence. There are a variety of antimicrobial products and there seems to be no clear way forward.

You are keen to conduct a review yourself but, sensibly, you first decide to see if there is one already out there in the literature. You search MEDLINE using PubMed Clinical Queries at www.ncbi.nlm.nih.gov/entrez/query/static/clinical.html. You type 'antimicrobial chronic wounds' in the query box of the Systematic Reviews feature and click the Go button. You find the following references, which are two reports of a relevant review:

- Systematic review of antimicrobial agents used for chronic wounds. *Br J Surgery* 2001; **88**: 4–21. (this review is based on the citation below)

Question components

The *population*: A clinically suitable sample of patients.

The *interventions*: Comparison of groups with and without the *intervention*.

The *outcomes*: Changes in health status due to *interventions*.

The *study design*: Ways of conducting research to assess the effect of *interventions*.

• Systematic review of wound care management: (3) antimicrobial agents for chronic wounds. *Health Technol Assess* 2000; **4**: 21. (available at www.hta.nhsweb.nhs.uk/htapubs.htm)

Step 1: Framing the question

Free form question

Which of the many available antimicrobial products improve healing in patients with chronic wounds?

Structured question (also see Boxes 1.2 and 1.3)

The *populations*   Adults with various forms of chronic wounds being cared for in an ambulatory setting. We narrow down the definition of chronic wounds to diabetic ulcer, venous ulcer, pressure ulcer and chronic ulcer (excluding pilonidal sinus – which was included in the related reviews – from further consideration in this case study).

The *interventions*   Systemic or topical antimicrobial preparations (eg antibiotics, antifungal, antiviral, anti-septic agents) compared with usual treatment, placebo or alternative antimicrobial products (excluding studies about prevention).

The *outcomes*   A range of assessment for wound healing, eg complete healing, change in ulcer size, rate of healing, time to heal, etc.

The *study designs*   Comparative studies with or without randomization (selection of non-randomized studies restricted to those with a concurrent control group).

Identifying relevant literature

• Develop search term combinations
• Search relevant electronic databases
• Search other relevant resources
• Select citations to retrieve potentially relevant papers
• Include/exclude studies using pre-set selection criteria

Step 2: Identifying relevant literature

A comprehensive search was undertaken by the reviewers (without language restrictions) to identify as many relevant published and unpublished studies as possible. The electronic search covered 17 databases from their inception to January 2000 (Box C3.1). The combination of search terms used for the MEDLINE database is shown in Box C3.2. Other databases were searched using a modified combination of these terms. In addition, manual searches of five relevant journals not covered by the electronic databases, 12 proceedings of relevant meetings and bibliographies of all retrieved articles were undertaken. A panel of subject experts was also consulted to identify studies

Box C3.1   Identification of relevant literature on antimicrobials for chronic wounds

Electronic databases searched*

1.   BIOSIS Previews (a database on life sciences)
2.   British Diabetic Association Database
3.   CINAHL (Cumulative Index of Nursing and Allied Health Literature);
4.   CISCOM (Computerised Information Service for Complementary Medicine)
5.   Cochrane Database of Systematic Reviews (CDSR)
6.   Cochrane Wounds Groups developing database
7.   Current Research in Britain (CRIB)
8.   Database of Abstracts of Reviews of Effectiveness (DARE)
9.   DHSS (Database produced by the Department of Health, UK on health services provided by the NHS nursing and primary care; people with disabilities and elderly people)
10.   Dissertation Abstracts
11.   EMBASE (Excerpta Medica Database)
12.   Index to Scientific and Technological Proceedings
13.   ISI® Science Citation Index
14.   MEDLINE (*see search term combinations in Box C3.2*)
15.   National Research Register (NRR)
16.   Royal College of Nursing Database
17.   System for Information on Grey Literature in Europe (SIGLE)

Study identification flow chart

Potentially relevant citations identified through comprehensive electronic searching of databases, hand searching and contact with experts

n = 400 citations with titles and abstracts

Citations excluded
n = 250

Retrival of hard copies of potentially relevant citations
n = 150 papers

Studies excluded after assessment of full text
n = 128

Studies included in systematic review
n = 22

Diabetic ulcers *n* = 3
Venous ulcers: *n* = 9
Pressure ulcers: *n* = 4
Chronic ulcers of mixed aetiologies: *n* = 6

* Economic evaluations were included in the original review, but as the question in this case study is concerned with effectiveness, we have not described them here

3

CASE

Box C3.2 Search term combination for Ovid MEDLINE database to identify citations on antimicrobials for chronic wounds

The original search term combination consists of 58 sets of terms. The following table shows only a selection of these. The purpose is to demonstrate how to build a search term combination.

Question components and relevant search terms	Type of terms Free	Type of terms MeSH	Boolean operator (*see glossary*)
The populations: patients with various forms of chronic wounds			
1 decubitus ulcer/ or foot ulcer		x	
2 leg ulcer/ or varicose ulcer/		x	
3 skin ulcer/		x	
4 diabetic foot/		x	
5 ((plantar or diabetic or heel or venous or stasis or arterial) adj ulcer).tw	x		OR (captures *population*)
6 ((decubitus or foot or diabetic or ischaemic or pressure) adj ulcer).tw	x		
7 ((pressure or bed) adj Sore$	x		
8 *additional terms (see in original report of the review)*			
9 or/1–8			
The interventions: treatments for chronic wounds			
10 debridement/ or biological dressings/ or bandages		x	
11 occlusive dressings/ or clothing/ or wound healing/		x	
12 antibiotics/ or growth substances/ or platelet-derived growth factor/		x	
13 (debridement or dressing$ or compress$ or cream$ or (growth adj factor$)).tw	x		OR (captures *intervention*)
14 antibiotic$ or (electric adj therapy) or laser$ or nutrition$ or surg$).tw	x		
15 (homeopath$ or acupuncture or massage or reflexology or ultrasound).tw	x		
16 *additional terms (see in original report of the review)*			
17 or/10–16			
The outcomes			
No search is performed to capture *outcomes*			
18 and/9,17			AND (combines *population* and *intervention*)
The study designs			
19 random allocation/ or randomized controlled trials/		x	
20 controlled clinical trials/ or clinical trials phase I/ or clinical trials phase II/		x	
21 single-blind method/ or double blind method/		x	OR (captures *study designs*)
22 ((random$ adj controlled adj trial$) or (prospective adj random$).tw.	x		
23 *additional terms (see in original report of the review)*			
24 or/19–23			

continued

Box C3.2   Search term combination for Ovid MEDLINE database to identify citations on antimicrobials for chronic wounds (*continued*)

Question components and relevant search terms	Type of terms		Boolean operator
	Free	MeSH	(*see glossary*)
25 18 and 24			AND (combines *population* and *intervention* and *study designs*)
26 limit 25 to human			

Commands and symbols for Ovid MEDLINE

/   Medical subject heading (MeSH) search, eg diabetic foot/ will search for MeSH in indexing terms

adj   Proximity and adjacency searching, eg growth adj factor$ means that these terms appear next to each other

.tw   Textword search, eg diabetic adj ulcer.tw will search for these adjacent textwords in title or abstract

$ Truncation, eg random$ will pick up words that start the same but have different endings, eg randomized, randomization, etc

The original search is part of the full report of the review available at

---

not captured by the searches. Examples of going to such great lengths to hunt down relevant literature are not as common in the field of systematic reviews as one might think. The initial search provides 400 possibly relevant citations. After screening their titles and abstracts, 150 papers are retrieved for examination of the full text. Despite the exhaustive efforts, ultimately only 22 studies (including over 1000 patients) are found that address the question posed.

Step 3: Assessing study quality

Study design threshold for study selection

From the outset, there was a worry that only a few studies with sound designs would be available. So the threshold for study selection had been lowered to allow observational studies with concurrent controls to be included along with randomized controlled trials and experimental studies without randomization (Box 1.4). Comparative studies with historical controls and case control studies were excluded because of the higher risk of bias associated with these designs (Box 2.4). Of the 22 studies selected, 18 claimed to be experimental studies (but only four were clearly randomized although with some deficiencies in concealment of allocation), and four were observational cohort studies with concurrent controls.

> The **quality** of a study depends on the degree to which its *design*, conduct and analysis minimizes **biases**.

3

CASE

Bias either exaggerates or underestimates the 'true' effect of an *intervention*.

Description of quality of the selected studies

The development of a quality checklist is outlined in Box C3.3. The selected studies are systematically examined for key generic biases: Is there potential for selection bias?, for performance bias?, for measurement bias? or for attrition bias? At the same time, quality issues specific to the *populations*, *interventions* and *outcomes* of the review question were considered. In this review, appropriateness of inclusion and exclusion criteria and comparability of groups at baseline for severity of ulcers was particularly important because there were concerns about inadequacies of methods used for minimizing selection bias. Assessment of the wound healing process to determine *outcomes* is critical even when measurement bias is minimized by blinding *outcome* assessors. This is because *outcome* assessment could be qualitatively different. For example, when assessing healing, the *outcomes* could be any one of complete healing, ulcer healing quotient, healing index, improvement scores, etc. Complete healing should be regarded as the most important *outcome* due to its importance to patients. Considering both generic and specific issues, a quality checklist with a total of nine items can be developed as shown in Box C3.3.

This checklist is applied to studies included in the review (Box C3.4), but the quality is often unclear due to lack of reporting. Where information on quality is available, many studies fall short of meeting the desired quality. For example, even when studies purport to be randomized, there are deficiencies both in sequence generation and in allocation concealment.

Step 4: Summarizing the evidence

A brief descriptive summary of the studies' characteristics and effects is tabulated in Box C3.5. A number of treatment comparisons were available but only in studies with a small number of patients (range 8–52 per group). Duration of follow-up also varied (range 2–20 weeks), and there was no consistency in measures of *outcomes*. This variation in what is done to whom, over what period and how *outcomes* are assessed, introduces clinical heterogeneity and this makes a meaningful synthesis of results difficult (and makes meta-analysis impossible).

Heterogeneity is the variation of effects between studies. It may arise because of differences between studies in key characteristics of their *populations*, *interventions* and *outcomes* (clinical heterogeneity), and their *study designs* and quality (methodological heterogeneity).

An examination of the observed effects in individual studies shows large values for point estimates of odds ratios (OR), but most effects are not statistically significant as the 95% confidence intervals (CI) include the possibility of no beneficial effect or even a harmful effect. For example, Wunderlich (1991) found that a silver-based product SIAX was better than various control regimens with an OR of 3.9 but the 95% CI is 0.7–22.1. Similarly, Alinovi (1986) showed that healing rate was worse when standard care was

---

Box C3.3   A quality assessment checklist for studies on effectiveness of antimicrobials for chronic wounds

The clinical question and selection criteria
- Nature of question   Assessment of effectiveness
- *Study design*   Evaluation of effectiveness of therapy, focussing on how one treatment compares with another (*see Box 1.4*)
- *Study design* threshold Inclusion criteria: randomized controlled trials (*see Box 2.4*)

    experimental studies without randomization

    cohort studies with concurrent controls

    Exclusion criteria: studies with historical controls

    case-control studies

The quality checklist
a) Generic quality items for checklist (see also Boxes 3.2 and 3.3)
- **Adequate generation of random sequence for allocating patients to interventions**
  Computer generated random numbers or random numbers tables
- **Adequate concealment of allocation**
  Robust methods to prevent foreknowledge of the allocation sequence to clinicians and patients, eg centralized real-time or pharmacy-controlled randomization in unblinded studies, or serially numbered identical containers in blinded studies
- **Adequate blinding**
  Care provider, study patients and outcome assessors
- ***A priori* sample size estimation**
- **Description of withdrawals**
  Numbers and reasons provided for each group
- **Intention-to-treat analysis (ITT)**

Inclusion of all those who dropped out/were lost to follow-up in the analysis so that the calculations indeed follow the ITT principle

b) Specific quality items related to clinical features of the review question
- **The *population***
  Correct inclusion/exclusion criteria
  Comparison of severity of wound condition at baseline
- **The *interventions***
  No items
- **The *outcome***

Hierarchy of outcomes (complete healing > ulcer healing quotient, healing index, improvement scores > microbial growth)

See Box C3.4 for description of study quality

3

supplemented by systemic antibiotics compared with standard care alone with an OR of 0.54, but 95% CI is 0.1–1.9. Even when effects were statistically significant, eg Morias (1979) reports OR 20.3 (95% CI 1.1–375.1), the estimation is quite imprecise

CASE

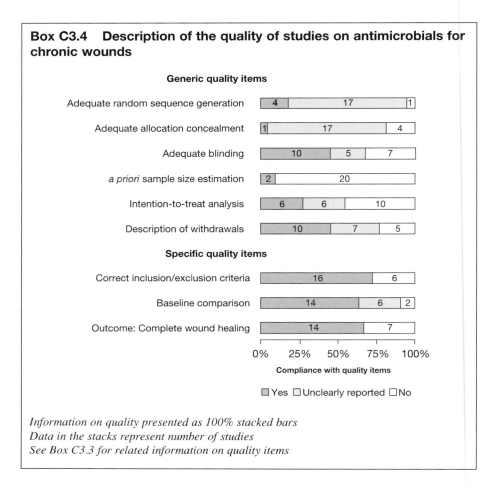

Box C3.4   Description of the quality of studies on antimicrobials for chronic wounds

Generic quality items

Adequate random sequence generation	4 / 17 / 1
Adequate allocation concealment	1 / 17 / 4
Adequate blinding	10 / 5 / 7
a priori sample size estimation	2 / 20
Intention-to-treat analysis	6 / 6 / 10
Description of withdrawals	10 / 7 / 5

Specific quality items

Correct inclusion/exclusion criteria	16 / 6
Baseline comparison	14 / 6 / 2
Outcome: Complete wound healing	14 / 7

0%   25%   50%   75%   100%

Compliance with quality items

■ Yes □ Unclearly reported □ No

Information on quality presented as 100% stacked bars
Data in the stacks represent number of studies
See Box C3.3 for related information on quality items

due to small sample size. Considering the low quality of the studies, one could hardly be enthused to trust such a result, even when it is statistically significant.

Power is the ability of a study to statistically demonstrate an effect when one exists. It is related to sample size. The larger the sample size, the more the power, and the lower the risk that a possible effect could be missed.

Step 5: Interpreting the findings

This review shows that research on the value of different antimicrobial products in wound care is scarce. Despite an exhaustive search effort, there are only a few relevant studies (Box C3.1) and their quality is relatively low (Box C3.4). A descriptive summary of the evidence shows that the observed effects are seemingly good (perhaps one reason why these studies are published despite their low quality), but they are imprecise, as insufficient numbers of patients are studied

(Box C3.5). Technically speaking, the studies are likely to be underpowered. In this situation, the studies are unable to detect an effect when one possibly exists, so one cannot prove the lack of effectiveness of the *interventions*. None of the numerous antimicrobials currently in use for various types of chronic ulcers have been robustly assessed, ie with appropriate design and conduct, clinically relevant *outcomes* and large enough sample size. Thus, no recommendations can be made regarding superiority or lack of effectiveness of any of the antimicrobial agents. Needless to say, additional research is needed.

Effect is a measure of association between an *intervention* and an *outcome*.

Point estimate of effect is its observed value in a study.

Confidence interval describes the imprecision in the point estimate, ie the range around it within which the 'true' value of the effect can be expected to lie with a given degree of certainty (95%). This reflects uncertainty due to play of chance.

Resolution of scenario

You are taken by surprise about the slim and feeble body of evidence on such a common problem as chronic wounds, which has a significant impact on healthcare resources in your primary healthcare setting. For you, it is currently not possible to inform a clinical policy on the management of chronic wounds with robust evidence.

Lack of evidence of effectiveness does not equate with evidence of lack of effectiveness! So you decide to form the most sensible policy using common sense and consensus of your colleagues (this keeps everyone happy). However, you obtain agreement to periodically seek new evidence and update your policy when new robust evidence becomes available.

To help fill the gap in evidence that you have identified through this review, there are some other options open to you. To help generate the new evidence:

- the least you can do is submit this topic to relevant research funding bodies for prioritisation
- you can also design and commence a robust clinical trial yourself if you are so inclined and obtain the funding to do this
- the most practical approach in our view is to actively recruit patients in a relevant clinical trial if there is one ongoing.

3

LIVERPOOL
JOHN MOORES UNIVERSITY
AVRIL ROBARTS LRC
TITHEBARN STREET
LIVERPOOL L2 2ER
TEL. 0151 231 4022

CASE

Box C3.5 A brief summary of the findings of studies included in a systematic review on antimicrobials for chronic wounds

(not all comparisons included in the original review are presented in this table)

Population subgroups	Interventions (number of patients/ulcers in group)		Outcomes		Effects
Study author & year of publication	Control group (standard/placebo)	Experimental group	Observation period	Outcome measure[+]	Effect estimate* (95% confidence interval)
Diabetic ulcer					
Systemic treatments					
Chanteleau 1996	Placebo (22)	Antibiotics (22)	3 weeks	Complete healing	OR: 0.45 (0.1–1.6)
Lipsky 1990	Cephalexin (29)	Clindamycin (27)	2 weeks	Complete healing	OR: 1.31 (0.4–4.0)
Topical treatments					
Vandeputte (unpublished)	Hydrogel (15)	Chlorhexidine (14)	12 weeks	Complete healing	OR: 0.07 (0.007–0.7)
Venous ulcer					
Systemic treatments					
Huovinen 1994	Ciprofloxacin (12)	Trimethoprim (12)	12 weeks	Complete healing	OR: 2.14 (0.38–12.2)
Alinovi 1986	Standard (24)	Antibiotics + standard (24)	3 weeks	Complete healing	OR: 0.54 (0.1–1.9)
Topical treatments					
Pierard-Franchimont 1997	Hydrocolloid (21)	Povidone iodine + hydrocolloid (21)	8 weeks	Median healing index	ES: 1.00 (−0.4–2.4)
Bishop 1992	Placebo (29)	Silver sulphadiazine (30)	4 weeks	Complete healing	OR: 7.57 (0.8–67.4)
Cameron 1991	Non-medicated tulle gras (15)	Mupirocin-impregnated tulle gras (15)	12 weeks	Complete healing	OR: 1.31 (0.31–5.49)
Salim 1991	Allopurinol (51)	Dimethyl sulphoxide (50)	12 weeks	Complete healing	OR: 2.04 (0.36–11.69)
Wunderlich 1991	Various preparations (20)	Silver impregnated activated charcoal dressing (20)	6 weeks	Complete healing	OR: 3.86 (0.7–22.1)
Blair 1988	Saline (30)	Silver sulphadiazine (30)	12 weeks	Complete healing	OR: 0.43 (0.14–1.38)
Pegum 1968	Lint (17)	Polynaxylin + lint (17)	Until healed	Mean ulcer healing quotient	ES: − 0.30 mm²/day (−2.1–1.5)

(continued)

Box C3.5 A brief summary of the findings of studies included in a systematic review on antimicrobials for chronic wounds *(continued)*

Population subgroups	Interventions (number of patients/ulcers in group)		Outcomes	Effects
Pressure ulcers	**Topical treatments**			
Della Marchina 1997	Alternative spray (10) Antiseptic spray (9)	15 days	Complete healing	OR: 2.57 (0.19–34.6)
Toba 1997	Povidone iodine/sugar (11) Gentian violet 0.1% blended with dibutyryl cAMP (8)	14 weeks	Mean % baseline ulcer area remaining	ES : 11.1 (−8.69–30.89)
Gerding 1992	A&D ointment (13) DermaMend (26)	4 weeks	No. of improved scores	OR: 6.57 (1.30–33.34)
Huchon 1992	Hydrocolloid (38) Povidone iodine (38)	8 weeks	Improved scores	OR: 0.46 (0.2–1.4)
Chronic ulcers of mixed aetiology	**Systemic treatments**			
Valtonen 1989	Disinfectant (8) Ciprofloxacin + Disinfectant (18)	12 weeks	Complete healing	OR: 3.84 (0.2–83.5)
Morias 1979	Placebo (29) Levamisole (30)	20 weeks	Complete healing	OR: 20.33 (1.1–375.1)
	Topical treatments			
Worsley 1991	Hydrocolloid (12) Povidone iodine ointment (15)	12 weeks	Complete healing	OR: 0.31 (0.05–2.08)
Beitner 1985	Saline (10) Benzoyl peroxide 20% (10)	6 weeks	Mean % remaining ulcer area	ES: 34.10 (21.1–47.1)
Margraf 1977	Various agents (10) Silver zinc allantoine cream (10)	Until healed	Mean days to heal	ES 59.0 (34.12–83.88)
Marzin 1982	Benzoyl peroxide (20) Collagen gel (20)	12 weeks	Wound area remaining	No effect estimate reported ($p<0.01$)

⁺ In studies with several outcome measures the most clinically important one is presented using the following hierarchy: complete healing > ulcer healing quotient, healing index, improvement scores > microbial growth.
* Odds ratio (OR) >1 and effect size (ES) >0 indicates improved *outcome* with experimental treatment.
See Box 4.1 for advice on constructing tables

3

CASE

Case study 4
Reviewing evidence on test accuracy

No document the size of this case study can purport to do justice to systematic reviews of test accuracy literature. We make no attempt to profess mastery of the methodological nuances in this expanding and, for some, exciting field.

In this case study, we reinforce the general principles behind systematic reviews by demonstrating their application in a scenario concerning use of evidence about accuracy of a test. It provides a good demonstration of exploration of heterogeneity, quantitative synthesis, subgroup meta-analysis and interpretation of findings.

Step 1
Framing questions

↓

Step 2
Identifying relevant literature

↓

Step 3
Assessing quality of
the literature

↓

Step 4
Summarizing the evidence

↓

Step 5
Interpreting the findings

Scenario: Ultrasound scan test for postmenopausal women with vaginal bleeding

You are a clinician responsible for women's health in a primary care centre serving a relatively large retired *population*. You are often faced with women who present with unexpected episodes of vaginal bleeding after menopause. You know that in the past these patients used to be routinely investigated by gynaecologists using uterine curettage under anaesthesia. This practice is now considered outdated, but current local practice still involves referral to a specialist based in a secondary care setting. You wonder if an ultrasound scan of the uterus can exclude pathology accurately in postmenopausal women with abnormal vaginal bleeding. In this way, women who test negative will not need referral to secondary care.

You search MEDLINE using PubMed Clinical Queries to see if there are any reviews in the literature. At www.ncbi.nlm.nih.gov/entrez/query/static/clinical.html you type 'ultrasound postmenopausal bleeding' in the query box of the Systematic Reviews feature and click the Go button. You find the following seemingly relevant citations on this topic:

- Evaluation of the woman with postmenopausal bleeding: Society of Radiologists in Ultrasound-Sponsored Consensus Conference statement. *J Ultrasound Med* 2001; **20**: 1025–36 (this is not a review).
- Ultrasonograpic measurement of endometrial thickness for diagnosing pathology in women with postmenopausal bleeding: A meta-analysis. *Acta Obstet Gynecol Scand* 2002; **81**: 799–816 (this seems to be the most up to date at the time of writing).

Question components

The *population*: A clinically suitable sample of patients

The *test*: The *test* whose predictive value is being assessed

The *reference standard*: A 'gold' standard test that confirms or refutes the diagnosis

The *study design*: Ways of conducting research to assess the predictive value of the *test*

Step 1: Framing the question

Free form question

Among postmenopausal women with abnormal vaginal bleeding, does pelvic ultrasound scan exclude uterine cancer accurately?

Structured question

The *population*	Postmenopausal women in the community with symptoms of vaginal bleeding.
The *test*	Endometrial thickness measurement during ultrasound imaging of the pelvis and the uterus (see Box C4.1). You are mainly interested in the accuracy of the negative *test* result.
The *reference standard*	Endometrial cancer confirmed histologically. There are many abnormalities of the endometrium and the uterus (benign, pre-cancer and cancer). Among your *population,* endometrial cancer is the most important one. Focusing on this diagnosis is not unreasonable (not least for the sake of simplicity in this case). You are mainly interested in excluding the diagnosis of cancer.
The *study design*	*Test* accuracy study (Box C4.3), ie observational studies in which results of a *test* (endometrial ultrasound) are compared with the results of a *reference standard* (endometrial histology).

Box C4.1   Ultrasound scan of the pelvis and the uterus

In ultrasound imaging of the uterus, the endometrium (lining of the womb) is described in terms of thickness and regularity. Regular endometrium with less than 5 mm thickness is often used to define a threshold or cut-off for abnormality. An example of a normal test result is shown below:

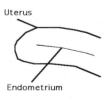

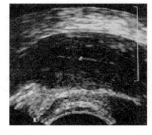

Step 2: Identifying relevant literature

An electronic search was carried out to capture all the relevant citations about ultrasound of the endometrium and then those citations that evaluate ultrasound among postmenopausal women with vaginal bleeding to predict the likelihood of endometrial cancer were identified. MEDLINE and EMBASE databases were searched without language restrictions. The search term combination included MeSH, textwords and appropriate word variants of '"ultrasound OR sonography" AND "endometrium OR uterus"'. The resultant set of citations was limited to human studies. The electronic search was coupled with manual scanning of bibliographies of known primary and review articles to identify relevant papers (Box C4.2). In total 57 studies (including 9031 patients) were included in the review. Of these, 21 studies were on the accuracy of endometrial thickness, at a 5mm abnormality threshold, to predict the diagnosis of endometrial cancer.

Identifying relevant literature
- Develop search term combinations
- Search relevant electronic databases
- Search other relevant resources
- Obtain full papers of potentially relevant citations
- Include/exclude studies using pre-set selection criteria

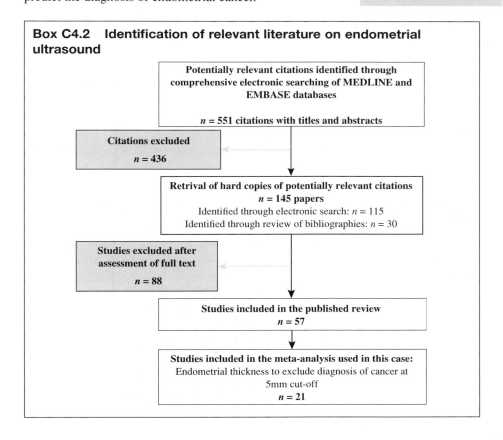

Box C4.2   Identification of relevant literature on endometrial ultrasound

Potentially relevant citations identified through comprehensive electronic searching of MEDLINE and EMBASE databases

n = 551 citations with titles and abstracts

Citations excluded
n = 436

Retrieval of hard copies of potentially relevant citations
n = 145 papers
Identified through electronic search: *n* = 115
Identified through review of bibliographies: *n* = 30

Studies excluded after assessment of full text
n = 88

Studies included in the published review
n = 57

Studies included in the meta-analysis used in this case:
Endometrial thickness to exclude diagnosis of cancer at 5mm cut-off
n = 21

4

CASE

Step 3: Assessing study quality

Quality assessment of test accuracy studies

An accuracy study is different from an effectiveness study. It is designed to generate a comparison between measurements obtained by a *test* and those obtained by a *reference standard*. A *reference standard* is a test that confirms or refutes the presence or absence of disease beyond reasonable doubt. Therefore it is sometimes also known as the 'gold' standard. We shall give a basic explanation about the *design* and quality features of a test accuracy study (Box C4.3).

> The **quality** of a study depends on the degree to which its *design*, conduct and analysis minimizes **biases**.

> **Bias** either exaggerates or underestimates the 'true' accuracy of a *test*.

There are many possible sources of bias in accuracy studies as shown in Box C4.3. Selection bias may arise if the sample is not suitably representative of the *population*. This is less likely to occur when using consecutive or random sampling. Poor descriptions of *test* and *reference standards* in terms of preparation of the patients, details of measurements, computation of results and thresholds for defining abnormality are also associated with bias. The *reference standard* should be a recognized 'gold' standard and it should be administered independent of the *test*. In addition, observers assessing *reference standards* for verification of diagnosis should be kept blind to measurements obtained from the *test*, and vice versa. Blinding avoids bias because recordings made by one observer are not influenced by the knowledge of the measurements obtained by other observers. During the verification process, bias may arise if the *reference standard* is not applied to all patients, or if it is differentially applied to *test*-positive and *test*-negative cases.

A detailed quality checklist is developed for assessment of test accuracy studies on endometrial ultrasound using the principles outlined in Step 3. We consider the elements of *study design* (generic items) and couple them with issues relevant to the review question (specific items), as shown in Box C4.3. An overview of the relevant generic aspects of test accuracy studies in this review reveals that the ultrasound *test* and the histological examination of the endometrium, which serves as the *reference standard*, are independent. So the remaining methodological issues related to recruitment of patients, blinding of observers and completeness of verification of diagnosis are examined.

Among quality issues related specifically to the review question, a sufficient description of the *population* to demonstrate that the sample is representative of the disease spectrum seen in practice is essential, otherwise the estimates of accuracy may not be applicable. For the *test*, *a priori* setting of the 5mm threshold is crucial, as post hoc determination of threshold is subject to manipulation in light of findings of the study. Finally, for the *reference standard*, use of adequate endometrial sampling is crucial to the validity of the selected studies. Adequate methods of obtaining endometrial samples include hysterectomy and directed biopsy.

Box C4.3 *Design* and quality of test accuracy studies evaluating endometrial ultrasound

Simple description of study design

An observational study that *tests* subjects from a relevant *population* and compares its results with those of a *reference standard*. For example, studies comparing results of endometrial ultrasound with those of endometrial histology in women with postmenopausal bleeding.

Study flowchart with key generic quality features

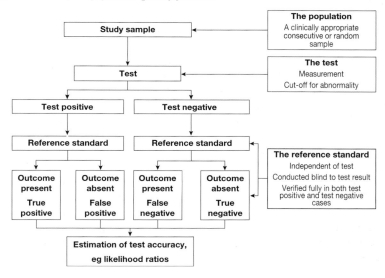

Development of a quality checklist

a) *Generic items obtained from the published research appraisal guidelines on test accuracy*
   - recruitment of subjects (consecutive or random sample)
   - independence between the test and the reference standard*
   - blinding of the observers conducting the reference standard to the findings of the test and vice versa
   - verification of diagnosis by reference standard in all tested cases.

b) *Specific items related to features of studies evaluating endometrial ultrasound*

The population	Appropriate spectrum composition
The test	Adequate description of endometrial ultrasound measurements determining cut-off level for abnormality *a priori*
The reference standard	Adequate endometrial samples obtained for reference standard histology. Hysterectomy and directed biopsy are adequate but blind (non-directed) biopsy may be less satisfactory.

*Not applicable in this review, see text for explanation

See Box C4.4 for results of quality assessment

4

CASE

Study design threshold for study selection

In this review a quality threshold in study selection was used to exclude all studies with case-control design. These studies would have selected cases with and without cancer and patients would have been retrospectively examined if their endometrial ultrasound scans were abnormal. Such a design has been empirically shown to be associated with bias leading to exaggeration of *test* accuracy.

Description of study quality for selected studies

Box C4.4 indicates the quality of selected studies. For most of the quality items, lack of compliance with good-quality features was due to lack of reporting. In general, there were deficiencies of one sort or another among all studies. The impact of these deficiencies on the estimation of accuracy is explored in Box C4.6.

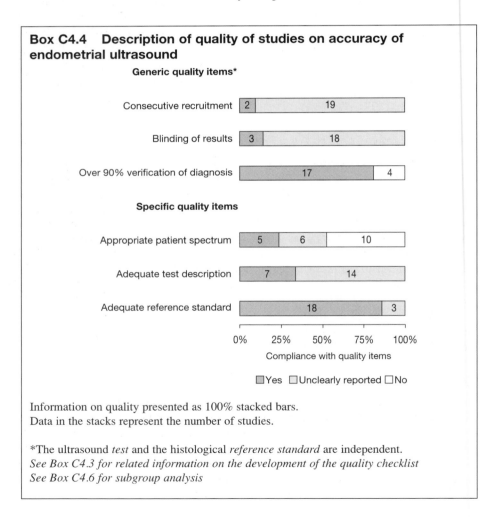

Box C4.4   Description of quality of studies on accuracy of endometrial ultrasound

Generic quality items*

Consecutive recruitment | 2 | 19

Blinding of results | 3 | 18

Over 90% verification of diagnosis | 17 | 4

Specific quality items

Appropriate patient spectrum | 5 | 6 | 10

Adequate test description | 7 | 14

Adequate reference standard | 18 | 3

0%   25%   50%   75%   100%
Compliance with quality items

☐Yes ☐Unclearly reported ☐No

Information on quality presented as 100% stacked bars.
Data in the stacks represent the number of studies.

*The ultrasound *test* and the histological *reference standard* are independent.
See Box C4.3 for related information on the development of the quality checklist
See Box C4.6 for subgroup analysis

Step 4: Summarizing the evidence

This case study describes the estimates of accuracy of individual studies, the examination of heterogeneity of accuracy across studies and the meta-analysis of individual accuracy estimates among studies using 5 mm thickness as the threshold for abnormality (other details of included studies can be obtained from the original report). But first we must understand how to choose a measure of accuracy (Box C4.5). The discussion about the pros and cons of various accuracy measures is a never-ending story in which there is no consensus among experts and is outside the remit of this book. To cut a long story short, meta-analysis with sensitivity and specificity is often considered to be of a limited clinical value. For the question posed in this case study, you are interested to discover the value of a negative endometrial ultrasound test (at a threshold of 5 mm thickness) for excluding endometrial cancer. Therefore, this case study limits its description of the statistical synthesis to the examination of individual likelihood ratios (LR) for negative *test* result and their meta-analysis.

Likelihood ratio (LR) is the ratio of the probability of a positive (or negative) *test* result in subjects with a disease to the probability of the same *test* result in subjects without the disease. The LR indicates by how much a given *test* result will raise or lower the probability of having the disease.

Variation in test accuracy from study to study

The point estimate of accuracy in each study, its precision (confidence interval) and the possibility of heterogeneity can be explored by examining variability of individual LRs in a forest plot. As shown in Box C4.6, there is a suspicion about heterogeneity, as confidence intervals do not overlap among some studies. Heterogeneity was confirmed by a formal statistical test. When heterogeneity was found its possible sources were searched for using subgroup analysis. Box C4.6 shows this approach for studies subgrouped according to their compliance with both generic and specific quality items. A similar subgroup analysis examined the impact of other study characteristics in the original report (not shown here). No explanation for heterogeneity could be found.

Heterogeneity is the variation between studies. It may arise because of differences between studies in key characteristics of their *populations*, *tests* and *reference standards* (clinical heterogeneity), and their *study designs* and quality (methodological heterogeneity).

Quantitative synthesis of results

In this instance heterogeneity remains unexplained despite an exhaustive exploration. Now do we, or do we not, perform meta-analysis? As discussed in Step 4, caution is required. In this review, authors chose to pool individual LRs using the random effects model (see Box 4.4). Precaution was taken to ensure that the summary point estimate was not biased by the choice of this method compared to a fixed effect model. In addition, lack of funnel plot asymmetry was assured to minimize the risk that publication and related biases impact on meta-analysis using random effects model.

CASE **4**

Box C4.5 Estimation of accuracy in studies evaluating *tests*

Measures of *test* accuracy

These are statistics for summarizing the accuracy of a *test*. For binary tests, there are three commonly used pairs of accuracy measures: positive and negative predictive values; sensitivity and specificity; and likelihood ratios. Unlike measures of effect, single measures of accuracy are infrequently used.

Computing accuracy for binary *test* results

A way of computing accuracy measures is shown below. Predictive values give the probability of having a disease and not having a disease among subjects with positive and negative *test* results respectively. Sensitivity and specificity give the probability of a positive and a negative test result among subjects with and without disease respectively. Likelihood ratios (LR) describe the relative probabilities of obtaining a test result in subjects with and without a disease. With several studies to compute accuracy for and to estimate uncertainty of the accuracy (its confidence intervals), manual calculations can become tedious. We would suggest using statistical software.

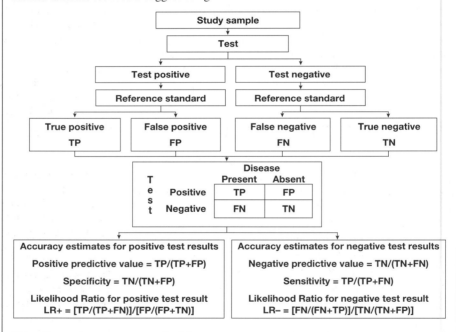

Choosing accuracy measures for binary *tests*

There is a debate about which measures are preferable and how best to pool them across several studies in a meta-analysis. No single approach is entirely satisfactory. Many experts consider pooling of predictive values, sensitivity and specificity inappropriate, as they do not behave independently. Without going into a long discussion about the pros and cons of various approaches, we admit our preference for LRs over other measures when a single threshold for abnormality is used in all studies. Likelihood ratios are more

continued

Box C4.5   Estimation of accuracy in studies evaluating *tests*
(*continued*)

clinically meaningful because when they are used in conjunction with information on disease prevalence (pre-*test* probability), they help to generate post-test probabilities as shown in Box C4.7. One word of caution: LRs are not suitable for pooling in meta-analysis when the threshold for abnormality varies from study to study. In this situation, a summary receiver operating characteristics plot allows for pooling of results from individual studies taking account of the relation between sensitivity and specificity.

See relevant sections of the Glossary for definitions of measures and methods of meta-analysis

---

Box C4.6 shows summary accuracy of the 21 studies evaluating the accuracy of endometrial ultrasound. A meta-analysis using the random effects model produced a summary LR- of 0.15 (95% CI 0.08–0.29). Interestingly the summary LR+ for positive test is 1.99 (95% CI 1.87–2.12) although this information is not really required to help with decision making in your case scenario.

Publication bias is said to arise when the likelihood of the publication of studies and thus their accessibility to reviewers is related to the significance of their results regardless of their quality.

Step 5: Interpreting the findings

The prevalence of endometrial cancer varies according to age. So the likelihood or probability of cancer given a negative ultrasound *test* result will also vary. The changes in probability produced by the summary LR- can be mathematically computed or they can be estimated using a nomogram (see Box C4.7). A negative *test* result virtually eliminates the possibility of endometrial cancer among younger women, however, it does not substantially reduce the probability among older women (in our view).

Pre-*test* probability is an estimate of probability of disease before *tests* are carried out. It is usually based on disease prevalence.

Post-*test* probability is an estimate of probability of disease in light of information obtained from testing. With accurate *tests*, the post-*test* estimates of probabilities change substantially from pre-*test* estimates.

Resolution of scenario

The answer to your question 'does a pelvic ultrasound scan exclude uterine cancer accurately in postmenopausal women with abnormal vaginal bleeding?' has to be 'yes, for many of your patients'. A negative result at <5 mm endometrial thickness rules out endometrial cancer with good certainty among low-risk patients (eg age <60 years), so there should be no need for you to refer them to tertiary care. It is important to remember that there is always a chance of a

117

4

CASE

LIVERPOOL JOHN MOORES UNIVERSITY
LEARNING SERVICES

Box C4.6   Exploring reasons for variation in accuracy among studies evaluating endometrial ultrasound

Forest plot

Summary of likelihood ratios for negative *test* results (LR-) among studies with an endometrial ultrasound *test* threshold of 5mm thickness (sorted in alphabetical order).

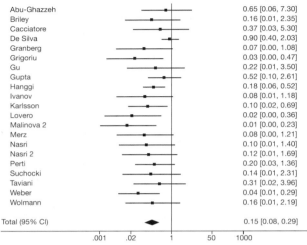

Abu-Ghazzeh	0.65 [0.06, 7.30]
Briley	0.16 [0.01, 2.35]
Cacciatore	0.37 [0.03, 5.30]
De Silva	0.90 [0.40, 2.03]
Granberg	0.07 [0.00, 1.08]
Grigoriu	0.03 [0.00, 0.47]
Gu	0.22 [0.01, 3.50]
Gupta	0.52 [0.10, 2.61]
Hanggi	0.18 [0.06, 0.52]
Ivanov	0.08 [0.01, 1.18]
Karlsson	0.10 [0.02, 0.69]
Lovero	0.02 [0.00, 0.36]
Malinova 2	0.01 [0.00, 0.23]
Merz	0.08 [0.00, 1.21]
Nasri	0.10 [0.01, 1.40]
Nasri 2	0.12 [0.01, 1.69]
Perti	0.20 [0.03, 1.36]
Suchocki	0.14 [0.01, 2.31]
Taviani	0.31 [0.02, 3.96]
Weber	0.04 [0.01, 0.29]
Wolmann	0.16 [0.01, 2.19]
Total (95% CI)	0.15 [0.08, 0.29]

Subgroup analyses according to study quality

The width of the diamond represents the confidence interval of LR- for subgroups of studies with particular quality characteristics. A vertical line in the centre of the diamond indicates the point estimate of the summary LR- for each subgroup. The point estimates of LRs vary. However, the confidence intervals of the summary LRs overlap, and it is not possible to find a clear explanation for heterogeneity.

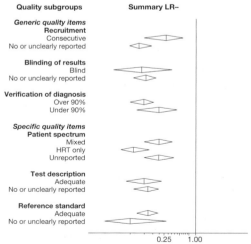

See Box C4.4 for related information on quality items

Box C4.7   The impact of a negative *test* result in endometrial ultrasound (at a 5 mm threshold) on the likelihood of endometrial cancer among postmenopausal women with vaginal bleeding

Generating post-*test* probabilities

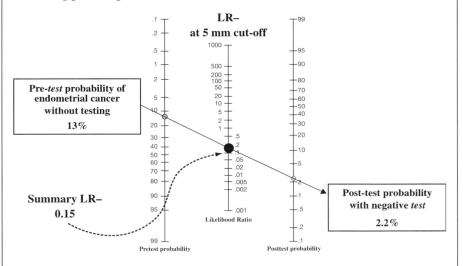

Nomogram adapted from *N Engl J Med* 1975; **293**: 257.
See Box C4.6 for summary likelihood ratio for negative test result, LR-

Post-*test* probabilities of endometrial cancer according to risk groups based on age

Age group	Pre-*test* probability*	Post-*test* probability[+]
<50 years	0.5%	0.1%
51–60 years	1.0%	0.2%
>60 years	13.0%	2.2%

* Obtained from population based data
[+] Computed using the following formula:

$$\text{Post-}test \text{ probability} = \frac{\text{Likelihood ratio} \times \text{Pre-}test \text{ probability}}{[(1 - \text{Pre-}test \text{ probability}) \times (1 - \text{Likelihood ratio})]}$$

false negative *test* result, even among low-risk patients. So, if patients remain symptomatic, they will need further evaluation. For high-risk patients (eg age >60 years) you don't have good certainty in ruling out disease from a negative ultrasound test, so you might even refer them on to secondary care without ultrasound testing. Needless to say, your low-risk patients with ultrasound endometrial thickness >5 mm would need to be investigated further in a secondary care setting to ascertain presence or absence of pathology.

CASE **4**

Suggested reading

This book focusses on core information about systematic reviews. The intricacies of many of the advanced techniques described briefly in this book, eg methods of meta-analysis, meta-regression analysis, funnel plot analysis, etc., can be examined in the materials referenced here.

Clarke M, Oxman A (eds). *Cochrane Reviewers' Handbook*. The Cochrane Collaboration, 2002.
  Available free at www.cochrane.dk/cochrane/handbook/handbook.htm

Egger M, Davey-Smith G, Altman DG (eds). *Systematic Reviews in Health Care. Meta-analysis in Context*. London: BMJ Publishing Group, 2001.
  Available at www.systematicreviews.com

Fletcher RH, Fletcher SW, Wagner EH. *Clinical Epidemiology: the Essentials. 3rd Edition*. Baltimore: Lippincott, Williams & Wilkins, 1996.

Glaziou P, Irwig L, Bain C, Colditz G. *Systematic Reviews in Health Care. A Practical Guide*. Cambridge: Cambridge University Press, 2001.

Khan KS, ter Riet G, Glanville J, Sowden AJ, Kleijnen J (eds) for the NHS Centre for Reviews and Dissemination (CRD). *Undertaking Systematic Reviews of Research on Effectiveness. CRD's Guidance for Carrying Out or Commissioning Reviews. 2nd Edition. CRD Report No. 4*. York: NHS Centre for Reviews and Dissemination, University of York, 2001.
  Available free at www.york.ac.uk/inst/crd/report4.htm

Mulrow CD, Cook D (eds). *Systematic Reviews. Synthesis of best evidence for Health Care Decisions*. Philadelphia, PA: American College of Physicians, 1998.

Sutton AJ, Abrams KR, Jones DR *et al*. Systematic Reviews of Trials and other studies. *Health Technology Assessment* 1998; **2(19)**; 1–276.
  Available free at www.ncchta.org/fullmono/mon219.pdf

Glossary

Absolute risk reduction (ARR)   see Risk difference (RD).

Accuracy measure   A statistic for summarizing the accuracy with which a test predicts a diagnosis or an outcome. There are three commonly used accuracy measures for binary tests: sensitivity and specificity; positive and negative predictive values; and likelihood ratios. All these measures are paired. Single measures of accuracy are seldom used with the exception of the diagnostic odds ratio.

Ascertainment bias   Systematic failure to ascertain exposures and outcomes adequately among all study participants. Also see Bias and Measurement bias.

Attrition bias (exclusion bias)   Systematic differences between study groups caused by exclusion or dropout of participants (eg because of side-effects of intervention) from the study. Intention-to-treat analysis in combination with appropriate sensitivity analyses including all participants can protect against this bias. Also see Bias, Intention-to-treat (ITT) analysis and Withdrawals.

Baseline risk   The rate of outcome in a population without an intervention. It is related to the severity of the underlying disease and other prognostic factors. Good prognosis is associated with a low baseline risk while poor prognosis is associated with a high baseline risk of undesirable outcomes. Baseline risk is important for determining who will benefit most from interventions. Also see Number needed to treat (NNT) and Prognosis.

Bias (systematic error)   A tendency for results to depart systematically, either lower or higher, from the 'true' results. Bias either exaggerates or underestimates the 'true' effect of an intervention or exposure. It may arise due to several reasons, eg errors in design and conduct of a study. This may lead to systematic differences in comparison groups (selection bias), differences in care or exposure to factors other than the intervention of interest (performance bias), differences in assessment of outcomes (measurement bias), withdrawals or exclusions of people entered into the study (attrition bias), etc. Studies with unbiased results are said to be internally valid.

Binary data   Measurement where the data have one of two alternatives, for example the patient is either alive or dead, the test result is either positive or negative, etc.

Blinding (masking)   Blinding keeps the study participants, caregivers, researchers and outcome assessors ignorant about the interventions to which the participants have been allocated in a study. In single blind studies only the participants are ignorant about interventions, but in double blind studies, both the participants and caregivers or researchers are blind. Outcome assessors can often be blinded even when participants and caregivers can't be. Blinding protects against performance bias and measurement bias, and it may contribute to adequate allocation concealment during randomization. Also see Randomization.

Boolean logic   Boolean logic (named after George Boole) refers to the logical relationship among search terms. Boolean operators AND, OR and NOT are used during literature searches to include or exclude certain citations from electronic databases. They are also used in Internet search engines.

Case-control study   A comparative observational study where participants/patients with the outcome (cases) and those without the outcome (controls) are compared for their prior intervention or exposure rates.

Clinical trial   A loosely defined term generally meaning to describe a study to evaluate efficacy and effectiveness of interventions. This term encompasses study designs ranging from randomized controlled trials to uncontrolled observations of a few cases.

Cochrane Collaboration   An international not-for-profit organization that aims to help with informed decision-making about health care by preparing, maintaining and improving accessibility of systematic reviews of interventions (www.cochrane.org). The major product of the Collaboration is the Cochrane Database of Systematic Reviews, which is part of the Cochrane Library (www.update-software.com/ cochrane/). Those who prepare Cochrane Reviews are mostly healthcare professionals who volunteer to work in one of fifty Collaborative Review Groups (CRGs). Each CRG has a coordinator and an editorial team to oversee the quality of their reviews. The activities of the Collaboration are directed by an elected Steering Group and are supported by staff in Cochrane Centres around the world.

Cohort study   A comparative observational study where participants with an intervention or exposure (not allocated by the researcher) are followed up to examine the difference in outcomes compared to a control group, eg those receiving no care or no exposure.

Comparative study   A study where the effect of an intervention or exposure is assessed using comparison groups. This can be a randomized controlled trial, a cohort study, a case-control study, etc.

Confidence interval (CI)   The range within which the 'true' value of a measurement (eg effect of an intervention) is expected to lie with a given degree of certainty. Confidence intervals represent the distribution probability of random errors, but not of systematic errors (bias). Conventionally, 95% confidence intervals are used.

Confounding   A situation in studies where the effect of an intervention on an outcome is distorted due to the association of the population and outcome with another factor, the confounding variable, which can prevent or cause the outcome independent of the intervention. It occurs when groups being compared are different with respect to important factors other than the interventions or exposures under investigation. Adjustment for confounding requires stratified or multivariable analysis. Also see Randomization.

Continuous data   Measurement on a continuous scale such as height, weight, blood pressure, etc. For continuous data, effect is often expressed in terms of mean difference. Also see Effect size (ES).

Control event rate (CER)   The proportion of participants in the control group in whom an event or outcome is observed during a defined time period.

Controlled clinical trial   A loosely defined term to describe a prospective comparative study for assessing efficacy of interventions (regardless of whether randomization is used or not). Watch out for indiscriminate use of this ambiguous term in reviews. It is also a MeSH in the MEDLINE database.

Cost effectiveness analysis   see Economic evaluation and Efficiency.

Diagnostic odds ratio   The ratio of the likelihood ratio for a positive test result to the likelihood ratio for a negative test result. It provides a single measure of accuracy. Also see Accuracy measure.

Economic evaluation (eg cost effectiveness analysis)   A study that takes into account both the clinical effectiveness and the costs of alternative interventions to address the question of how to achieve an optimal clinical outcome at the lowest cost. The term 'cost effectiveness analysis' is often used synonymously, but this is a misnomer. A full economic evaluation considers both clinical and cost outcomes, whereas a partial evaluation may only consider costs without regard to clinical outcomes. Also see Efficiency.

Effect (effect measure, treatment effect, estimate of effect, effect size)   Effect is the observed association between interventions and outcomes or a statistic to summarize the strength of the observed association. The statistic could be a relative risk, odds ratio, risk difference, or number needed to treat for binary data; a mean difference, or standardized mean difference for continuous data; or a hazard ratio for survival data. The effect has a point estimate and a confidence interval. The term *individual effect* is often used to describe effects observed in individual studies included in a review. The term *summary effect* is used to describe the effect generated by pooling individual effects in a meta-analysis.

Effect modifier   A factor influencing the effect of the intervention under study, eg age may modify responsiveness to treatment.

Effect size (ES)   This term is sometimes used for an effect measure for continuous data. In social and psychological sciences it is the same as standardized mean difference. Also see Effect measure, Mean difference and Standarized mean difference.

Effectiveness   The extent to which an intervention (therapy, prevention, diagnosis, screening, education, social care, etc.) produces a beneficial outcome in the routine setting. Unlike efficacy, it seeks to address the question: Does an intervention work under ordinary day-to-day circumstances?

Efficacy   The extent to which an intervention can produce a beneficial outcome under ideal circumstances.

Efficiency   The extent to which the balance between input (costs) and outputs (outcomes) of interventions represents value for money. It addresses the question of whether clinical outcomes are maximized for the given input costs. Also see Economic evaluation.

Evidence-based medicine (EBM)   The conscientious, explicit and judicious use of current best evidence in making decisions about the care of individual patients. It involves the process of systematically finding, appraising and using contemporaneous research findings as the basis for clinical decisions. Evidence-based practice (EBP) is a related term. Both EBM and EBP follow four steps: formulate a clear clinical question from a patient's problem; search the literature for relevant clinical articles; evaluate (critically appraise) the evidence for its validity and usefulness; implement useful findings in clinical practice taking account of patients' preferences and caregivers' experience. Another related term is evidence-based health care, which is an extension of the principles of EBM to all professions associated with health care, including purchasing and management. Systematic reviews provide powerful evidence to support all forms of EBM.

Experimental event rate (EER)   The proportion of participants in the experimental group in whom an event or outcome is observed during a specified time period.

Experimental study   A comparative study in which decisions concerning the allocation of participants or patients to different interventions are under the control of the researcher, eg randomized controlled trial.

Exposure   A factor (including interventions) which is thought to be associated with the development or prevention of an outcome.

External validity (generalizability, applicability)   The extent to which the effects observed in a study can be expected to apply in routine clinical practice, ie to people who did not participate in the study. Also see Validity.

Fixed effect model   A statistical model for combining results of individual studies. It assumes that the effect is truly constant in all the populations studied. Thus, only within-study variation is taken to influence the uncertainty of the summary effect and it produces narrower confidence intervals than the random effects model. Also see Random effects model.

Forest plot   A graphical display of individual effects observed in studies included in a systematic review (along with the summary effect if meta-analysis is used).

Funnel plot   A scatter plot of effects observed in individual studies included in a systematic review against some measure of study information, eg study size, inverse of variance, etc. It is used in exploration for the risk of publication and related biases.

Guidelines   Systematically developed statements that aim to assist practitioners and patients in making decisions about specific clinical situations. They often, but not always, use evidence from systematic reviews.

Hazard ratio   An effect measure for survival data, which compares the survival experience of two groups.

Health technology assessment (HTA)   Health technology includes any method used by those working in health services to promote health; to screen, diagnose, prevent and treat disease; and to improve rehabilitation and long-term care. HTA considers the effectiveness, appropriateness, costs and broader impact of interventions using both primary research and systematic reviews.

Heterogeneity/Homogeneity   The degree to which the effects among individual studies being systematically reviewed are similar (homogeneity) or different (heterogeneity). This may be observed graphically by examining the variation in individual effects (both point estimates and confidence intervals) in a Forest plot. Quantitatively, statistical tests of heterogeneity/homogeneity may be used to determine if the observed variation in effects is greater than that expected due to the play of chance alone. For making a clinical judgement about heterogeneity, one might look at the differences between populations, interventions and outcomes of studies. Also see Subgroup analysis

Homogeneity   see Heterogeneity.

Intention-to-treat (ITT) analysis   An analysis where participants are analysed according to their initial group allocation, independent of whether they dropped out or not, fully complied with the intervention or not, or crossed over and received alternative interventions. A true ITT analysis includes an outcome (whether observed or estimated) for all patients. Also see Attrition bias and Sensitivity analysis.

Internal validity   see Validity.

Intervention   A therapeutic or preventative regimen, eg a drug, an operative procedure, a dietary supplement, an educational leaflet, a test (followed by a treatment), etc. undertaken with the aim of improving health outcomes. In a randomized trial, the effect of an intervention is the comparison of outcomes between two groups, one with the intervention and the other without (eg a placebo or another control intervention).

Inverse of variance   see Variance.

Likelihood ratio (LR)   It is the ratio of the probability of a positive (or negative) test result in participants with a disease to the probability of the same test result in participants without the disease. The LR indicates by how much a given test result raises or lowers the probability of having the disease. With a positive test result, a LR+ >1 increases the probability that disease will be present. The greater the LR+ the larger the increase in probability of the disease and the more clinically useful the test result. With a negative test result, a LR- <1 decreases the probability that the disease is present. The smaller the LR-, the larger the decrease in the probability of disease and the more clinically useful the test result.

Mean difference The difference between the means (ie the average values) of two groups of measurements on a continuous scale. Also see Effect, Standardized mean difference (SMD) and Weighted mean difference (WMD).

Measurement bias (detection bias, ascertainment bias)   Systematic differences between groups in how exposures and outcomes are ascertained in a study. Blinding of study participants and outcome assessors protects against this bias. Also see Bias.

MeSH   Medical Subject Heading. Controlled terms used in the MEDLINE database to index citations. Other electronic bibliographic databases frequently use MeSH-like terms.

Meta-analysis   A statistical technique for combining (pooling) the results of a number of studies that address the same question to produce a summary result.

Meta-regression   A multivariable model with effect estimates of individual studies (usually weighted according to their size) as dependent variable and various study characteristics as independent variables. It searches for the influence of study characteristics on the size of effects observed in a systematic review. Also see Multivariable analysis.

Multivariable analysis (multivariable model) An analysis that relates some independent or explanatory or predictor variables $(X1, X2, ...)$ to a dependent or outcome variable (Y) through a mathematical model such as $Y = \beta0 + \beta1X1 + \beta2X2 + ...$, where Y is the outcome variable; $\beta0$ is the intercept term; and $\beta1, \beta2, ...$ are the regression coefficients indicating the impact of the independent variables $X1, X2, ...$ on the dependent variable Y. The coefficient is interpreted as the change in the outcome variable associated with a one-unit change in the independent variable and provides a measure of association or effect. Multivariable analysis is used to adjust for confounding, eg by including confounding factors along with the intervention (or exposure) as the independent variables in the model. This way the effect of intervention (or exposure) on outcome can be estimated while adjusting for the confounding effect of other factors. Also see Confounding.

Negative predictive value The proportion of study participants who test negative who truly do not have the disease.

Normal distribution A frequency distribution that is symmetrical around the mean and is bell-shaped (also called Gaussian distribution).

Null hypothesis The hypothesis put forward when carrying out significance tests that states that there is no difference between groups in a study. For example, statistically we discover that an intervention is effective by rejecting the null hypothesis that outcomes are not different between the experimental and the control group. Also see *p*-value.

Number needed to harm (NNH) It is the number of patients treated for whom there is one additional patient who experiences an episode of harm (adverse effect, complication, etc.). It is computed in the same manner as NNT.

Number needed to treat (NNT) An effect measure for binary data. It is the number of patients who need to be treated to prevent one undesirable outcome. In an individual study it is the inverse of risk difference (RD). In a systematic review it is computed using baseline risk and a measure of relative effect (relative risk, odds ratio). It is a clinically intuitive measure of the impact of a treatment.

Observational study Research studies in which interventions, exposures and outcomes are merely observed with or without control groups. These could be cohort studies, case-control studies, cross-sectional studies, etc.

Odds The ratio of the number of participants with an outcome to the number without the outcome in a group. Therefore, if out of 100 participants 30 had the outcome and 70 did not, the odds would be 30/70 or 0.42. Also see Risk.

Odds ratio (OR) An effect measure for binary data. It is the ratio of odds of an event or outcome in the experimental group to the odds of an outcome in the control group. An OR of 1.0 indicates no difference between comparison groups. For undesirable outcomes an OR that is less than 1.0 indicates that the intervention is effective in reducing the odds of that outcome. Also see Relative risk.

Outcome The changes in health status that arise from interventions or exposure. The results of such changes are used to estimate the effect.

p - value (statistical significance) The probability, given a null hypothesis, that the observed effects or more extreme effects in a study could have occurred due to play of chance (random error). In an effectiveness study, it is the probability of finding an effect by chance as unusual as, or more unusual than, the one calculated, given that the null hypothesis is correct. Conventionally, a *p*-value of less than 5% (ie $p<0.05$) has been regarded as statistically significant. This threshold, however, should never be allowed to become a straight jacket. When statistical tests have low power, eg tests for heterogeneity, a less stringent threshold (eg $p<0.1$ or <0.2) may be used. Conversely, when there is a risk of spurious significance, eg multiple testing in subgroup analysis, a more stringent threshold (e.g. $p<0.01$) may be used. When interpreting the significance of effects, *p*-values should always be used in conjunction with confidence intervals (CI). Also see Confidence interval.

Performance bias Systematic differences in the care provided to the study participants apart from the interventions being evaluated. Blinding of carers and participants and standardization of the care plan can protect against this bias. Also see Bias.

Point estimate of effect The observed value of the effect of an intervention among the participants in a study sample. Also see Confidence interval (CI).

Positive predictive value The proportion of study participants who test positive and who truly have the disease.

Post-test probability of disease An estimate of the probability of disease in light of the information obtained from testing. With accurate tests, the post-test estimates of probabilities change substantially from pre-test estimates. In this way a positive test result may help to rule in disease and a negative test result may help to rule out disease.

Power The ability to demonstrate an association when one exists. The ability to reject the null hypothesis when it is indeed false. Power is related to sample size; the larger the sample size, the greater the power and the lower the risk that a possible association could be missed.

Precision (specificity) of a search The proportion of relevant studies identified by a search strategy expressed as a percentage of all studies (relevant and irrelevant) identified by that method. It describes the ability of a search to exclude irrelevant studies. Also see Sensitivity of a search.

Precision of effect see Random error.

Pre-test probability of disease An estimate of probability of disease before tests are carried out. It is usually estimated as the prevalence of a disease in a given setting (eg community, primary care, secondary care, hospital, etc.). Sometimes, when such information is not available, it may have to be guessed.

Prognosis A probable course or outcome of a disease. Prognostic factors are patient or disease characteristics which influence the course. Good prognosis is associated with a low rate of undesirable outcomes; poor prognosis is associated with a high rate of undesirable outcomes. Also see Baseline risk.

Publication bias   Arises when the likelihood of publication of a study is related to the significance of its results. For example, a study is less likely to be published if it finds an intervention ineffective. Reviewers should make all efforts to identify such negative studies otherwise their inferences about the value of intervention will be biased. Funnel plots may be used to explore for the risk of publication and related biases.

Qualitative research   Research concerned with the subjective world that offers insight into social, emotional and experiential phenomena in health and social care. Including findings from qualitative research may enhance the quality and salience of reviews.

Quality of a study (methodological quality)   The degree to which a study minimizes biases. Features related to the design, the conduct and the statistical analysis of the study can be used to measure quality. This determines the validity of results.

Quasi-experimental (quasi-randomized) study   A term sometimes used to describe a study where allocation of participants to different groups is controlled by the researcher, like in an experimental study, but the method falls short of genuine randomization (and allocation concealment), eg by using date of birth or even/odd days. One should interpret the term 'quasi' carefully because studies of this kind may be of poor quality.

Random effects model   A statistical model for combining the results of studies that allows for variation in the effect among the populations studied. Thus, both within-study variation and between-studies variation are included in the assessment of the uncertainty of results. Also see Fixed effect model.

Random error (imprecision or sampling error)   Error due to the play of chance that leads to confidence intervals around the point estimates of effect. The width of the confidence interval reflects the magnitude of random error or imprecision. Also see *p*-value.

Randomization (with allocation concealment)   Randomization is the allocation of study participants to two or more alternative groups using a chance procedure, such as computer generated random numbers, to generate a sequence for allocation. It ensures that participants have a prespecified (very often an equal) chance of being allocated to one of two or more interventions. In this way the groups are likely to be balanced for known as well as unknown and unmeasured confounding variables. Concealment of the allocation sequence until the time of allocation to groups is essential for protection against selection bias. Foreknowledge of group allocation leaves the decision to recruit the subject open to manipulation by researchers and study participants themselves. Allocation concealment is almost always possible even when blinding is not. Randomization alone without concealment does not protect against selection bias.

Randomized controlled trial (RCT)   A comparative study with random allocation (with allocation concealment) of participants to intervention groups, and follow-up to examine differences in outcomes between the various groups.

Relative Risk (RR) (risk ratio, rate ratio)   An effect measure for binary data. It is the ratio of risk in the experimental group to the risk in the control group. An RR of 1.0

indicates no difference between comparison groups. For undesirable outcomes an RR that is less than 1.0 indicates that the intervention is effective in reducing the risk of that outcome. Also see Odds ratio.

Review An article that summarizes the evidence contained in a number of different individual studies and draws conclusions about their findings. It may or may not be systematic. Also see Systematic Review and Meta-analysis.

RevMan The Cochrane Collaboration's software for review management and meta-analysis (available at www.cochrane.org/cochrane/revman.htm).

Risk (proportion or rate) The proportion of participants in a group who are observed to have an outcome. If out of 100 participants, 30 had the outcome, the risk (rate of outcome) would be 30/100 or 0.30. Also see Odds.

Risk difference (RD) (absolute risk reduction, rate difference) An effect measure for binary data. In a comparative study it is the difference in event rates between two groups. The inverse of RD produces number needed to treat. Also see Number needed to treat (NNT).

Safety Adverse events and harmful outcomes associated with interventions or exposures. Systematic reviews on the safety of interventions or exposures should consider including studies of both experimental and observational designs. This is because experimental studies are usually of short duration and typically assess only a small number of patients; thus the chances of detecting rare adverse events are small.

Sample Participants selected for a study from a group or population.

Selection bias (allocation bias) Systematic differences in prognosis and/or therapeutic sensitivity at baseline between study groups. Randomization (with concealed allocation) of patients protects against this bias.

Sensitivity analysis Repetition of an analysis under different assumptions to examine the impact of these assumptions on the results. In systematic reviews, when there is poor reporting in individual studies, authors of primary studies should be asked to provide missing and unclear information. However, this is not always possible and reviewers often have to make assumptions about methods and data and they may impute missing information. In this situation, a sensitivity analysis should be carried out, involving a reanalysis of the review's findings and taking into account the uncertainty in the methods and the data. This helps to determine if the inferences of a systematic review change due to these uncertainties. In a primary study there may be withdrawals, so sensitivity analysis may involve repeating the analysis, imputing the best or worst outcome for the missing observations or carrying forward the last outcome assessment. Also see Intention-to-treat analysis (ITT) and Withdrawals.

Sensitivity (recall) of a search The proportion of relevant studies identified by a search strategy expressed as a percentage of all relevant studies on a given topic. It describes the comprehensiveness of a search method, ie its ability to identify all relevant studies on a given topic. Highly sensitive strategies tend to have low levels of precision and vice versa. Also see Precision of a search.

Sensitivity (true positive rate) of a test   The proportion of those people who really have the disease and who are correctly identified as such.

Specificity (true negative rate) of a test   The proportion of those participants who really do not have disease and who are correctly identified as such.

Standardized mean difference (SMD)   An effect measure for continuous data where studies have measured an outcome using different scales (eg pain may be measured in a variety of ways). The mean difference is divided by an estimate of the within-group variance to produce a standardized value without any units. Also see Effect and Effect size.

Statistical significance   see *p*-value.

Subgroup analysis (in systematic reviews)   Meta-analyses may be carried out in pre-specified subgroups of studies stratified according to differences in populations, interventions, outcomes and study designs. This allows reviewers to determine if the effects of an intervention vary between subgroups.

Summary receiver operating characteristics curve (SROC)   A method of summarizing the performance of a dichotomous test pooling 2×2 tables from multiple studies or multiple cut-off points. It takes into account the relationship between sensitivity and specificity among the individual studies by plotting the true positive rate (sensitivity) against the false positive rate (1-specificity).

Systematic error   *see* Bias.

Systematic review (systematic overview)   Research that summarizes the evidence on a clearly formulated question using systematic and explicit methods to identify, select and appraise relevant primary studies, and to extract, collate and report their findings. By following this process it becomes a proper piece of research. It may or may not use statistical meta-analysis.

Trial   see Clinical trial.

Validity (internal validity)   The degree to which the results of a study are likely to approximate the 'truth' for the participants recruited in a study, ie are the results free of bias? It refers to the integrity of the design and is a prerequisite for applicability (external validity) of a study's findings. Also see External validity.

Variance   A statistical measure of variation measured in terms of the deviations of individual observations from the mean value. The inverse of variance of the observed individual effects is often used to weight studies in statistical analyses used in systematic reviews, eg meta-analysis, meta-regression and funnel plot analysis.

Weighted mean difference   A summary effect measure for continuous data where studies that have measured the outcome on the same scales (eg height) have been pooled. Also see Effect.

Withdrawals   Participants or patients who do not fully comply with the intervention, cross over and receive an alternative intervention, choose to drop out, or are lost to follow-up. Also see Attrition bias, Intention-to-treat analysis (ITT) and Sensitivity analysis.

Index